ISD
INSTRUCTIONAL
SYSTEMS DESIGN

Robert R. Carkhuff and
Sharon G. Fisher

with

John R. Cannon,
Theodore W. Friel, and
Richard M. Pierce

Human Resource Development Press, Inc.
Publishers of Human Technology

Copyright © 1984 by
Human Resource Development Press, Inc.

22 Amherst Rd.
Amherst, Massachusetts 01002 (413) 253-3488

Bernice R. Carkhuff, Publisher

First Edition, First printing, January, 1984
            Second printing, October 1985
Library of Congress Catalog #84-196323
International Standard Book Number 0-914234-72-2

Cover Art by Krawczyk
Cover Design by Tom Bellucci
Composition by Jean Miller
Printing and Binding by Bookcrafters

TABLE OF CONTENTS

About The Authors

Robert R. Carkhuff, Ph.D., Chairman, Carkhuff Institute of Human Technology, Amherst, Massachusetts, is among the most-cited social scientists according to the Institute for Scientific Information. He is author of three of the most-referenced social science texts, including two volumes on *"Helping and Human Relations."* His latest books are *"Sources of Human Productivity"* and *"The Exemplary Performer in the Age of Productivity."*

Sharon G. Fisher, M.Ed., Director, Instructional Systems Design, Human Technology, Inc., McLean, Virginia, has designed hundreds of public and private sector instructional projects and products. She is recipient of the first "Exemplar Award" for her exemplary products in C.A.I. as well as print material.

John R. Cannon, Ph.D., Director, Management Systems, Human Technology, Inc., McLean, Virginia, has directed more than 600 projects in the last 12 years. He is co-author of a forthcoming book on *"The Art and Science of Consulting."*

Richard M. Pierce, Ph.D., Director, Human Resource Development, Human Technology, Inc., McLean, Virginia, has designed the implementation programs for more than 500 projects in the last 15 years. He is co-author of a forthcoming book on *"Performance Management Systems."*

Theodore W. Friel, Ph.D., Director, Advanced Systems Design, Human Technology, Inc., McLean, Virginia, has done operations planning for more than 400 projects in the last 14 years. He is author of *"The Art of Developing a Career"* and co-author of a forthcoming book on *"Human Resource Planning."*

Preface

Historically, evaluation has been thought of as the province of research scientists and statisticians. Training and development personnel often shied away from systematic assessments of their endeavors.

As the Age of Productivity moves us toward comprehensive designs for systematic instructional interventions (see ISD Volume I), we must also move toward comprehensive designs for the evaluation of instructional interventions.

Our instructional interventions must be designed to achieve multiple levels of impact, from recipient process involvement through organizational productivity outcomes. In like manner, our instructional evaluations must be designed to insure the systematic assessment of all the intended levels of impact.

Volume II of ISD presents the tools that training and development professionals need to design comprehensive and systematic evaluations of productivity-focused instructional interventions. These tools are organized within the following major tasks:

- Assessing Process Movement
- Assessing Content Acquisition
- Assessing Skill Application
- Assessing Task Transfer
- Assessing Goal Achievement

It is the accomplishment of these tasks that enables us to demonstrate, in concrete terms, the responsibility, accountability and productivity of our instructional endeavors.

R.R.C.
S.G.F.

Washington, D.C.
January 1984

Foreword

Robert R. Carkhuff and his associates are to human processing what Jack Kilby and his associates were to computer processing. Kilby brought us the microprocessor and, in so doing, introduced the Age of Information Processing. Carkhuff brought us training and learning strategies and, in so doing, introduced the Age of Human Productivity.

We in information processing have long recognized the need for "thinking humans" to drive our information systems. Now we have the vehicles for training the thinking humans. Moreover, now we have the vehicles for transforming their thought processes into organizational productivity.

Carkhuff, Fisher, Cannon, Friel, and Pierce bring us the distillation of their own processing on instructional systems design. Beginning with the missions of the decision-makers, they teach us how to transform these missions into measurable productivity improvements. Volume I provides us with the skills of designing instructional systems. Volume II offers us the skills of evaluating instructional systems. Together, they provide a comprehensive picture of the place of education and training in productivity systems design.

The models, systems, and skills are not only totally innovative and fluidly communicative, they are also presented in an information-simplified manner, with abundant job aids and illustrations. The authors demonstrate the power of their own productivity in their products. They have given order and potency to a once-chaotic area.

The core of *ISD* remains the operations at the various stations. In Volume I, the authors teach us how to analyze tasks, define training objectives, and develop content and training plans. In Volume II, they teach us how to use a criterion-referenced approach to evaluation. Their mode of teaching is highly operational and highly useful. Above all, it is logical, simple and straight-forward.

These *ISD* volumes enable us to make a multitude of applications in our daily operations in the private sector. No longer do we require six months to design a training program that is already obsolete. We can now make immediate contributions to immediate needs. To be sure, we can design instructional systems to achieve any human goal in business or government or, for that matter, in our homes and in our schools.

To sum, these two volumes on instructional design teach us how to transform the smallest value in a decision-maker's head into a productive training delivery. They are a necessary resource for every manager of human resources and every developer and deliverer of education and training.

In short, Carkhuff and his associates teach us that we get what we train for—no more, no less! Our training productivity will be as productive as our instructional design is systematic. These volumes teach us how to develop and evaluate these systematic designs. *ISD* is clearly the most systematic approach to training design.

Jack Kelly
Manager, Human Resources
Information Systems Technology Group
International Business Machines

INTRODUCTION

THE PRODUCTIVE INTERVENTION: A CASE STUDY

An Industrial Relations (IR) Department of a multinational corporation was responsible for productivity improvement through human and information resource development. IR policy makers established a new mission of providing productivity improvement services throughout the corporation. In other words:

> **EXTERNAL MISSION:** To market and deliver productivity improvement services to other Departments within the corporation and other corporations.

CONSULTING DESIGN

The expansion of the IR Department's mission was viewed as an R & D effort. A special cost center was established for tracking the costs and benefits generated by the productivity improvement program (PIP). To gain full corporate acceptance of PIP, it was essential that the IR Department prepare its own personnel for such a mission. In other words, IR needed to improve the performance of its individual personnel and the overall productivity of its own Department in order to be successful.

> **INTERNAL MISSION:** To improve the performance of IR consultants.

The burden of the performance improvement efforts falls upon the resource component within IR. The strategic goal was to improve the performance of IR resources while reducing the resource expenditures.

> **STRATEGIC GOAL:** To increase individual IR staff performance outcomes by 10%, while reducing resource expenditures by 5%.

IR's resource component needed to make strategic decisions concerning the alternative courses of actions to be used in order to reach the strategic goal. Basically, IR had to choose between increasing its internal capacity through hiring and firing or developing its internal capacity through training. Employing the productivity values of the policy makers, the IR resource component decided that developing its internal capacity was the most cost beneficial course of action.

> **STRATEGIC DECISION:** To develop the internal consulting capacity through personnel training.

Accordingly, strategic plans were developed for implementing the selected course of action. The strategic plans detailed the instructional design tasks to be performed.

> **STRATEGIC PLANS:** To develop instructional systems design to train IR personnel.

INSTRUCTIONAL DESIGN

The strategic plan was delivered to the decision makers. After consideration, the decision makers refined the plan by recycling the strategic decisions, goals, and mission. The instructional system design (ISD) was initiated by establishing the productivity goals for the personnel to be trained.

> **ISD PRODUCTIVITY GOAL:** To improve the quantity and quality of individual consulting performance by 10% or more.

In order to improve individual performance, the instructional technologist needed to analyze the tasks that the personnel would be required to perform. This analysis emphasized the processing of the inputs into outputs. It also included the enabling tasks that overcame the barriers to the performance of process tasks.

> **PERSONNEL TASKS:** To process consulting inputs more efficiently and consulting outputs more effectively.

The training objectives emphasized the skills the personnel needed in order to perform their consulting tasks more productively. The objectives emphasized the skills that underlie planning, producing, and assessing tasks. These skills became the training objectives.

> **TRAINING OBJECTIVES:** To apply skills underlying planning, producing, and assessing to consulting tasks.

The training content flowed directly from the training objective. It emphasized the skill steps and supportive knowledge which the personnel would require to perform the planning, producing, and assessing skills.

> **CONTENT OUTCOMES:** To acquire the skill steps and supportive knowledge required to perform the planning, producing, and assessing skills.

A training delivery plan was developed. It organized the training content to facilitate the training delivery. It emphasized the training methods that insured learning.

> **DELIVERY OUTCOMES:**   To organize the content and methods to insure trainee learning.

Finally, the training delivery was made. The trainers emphasized both the requirements of the content and the experiences of the trainees in making the training delivery. The ISD personnel now needed to assess the efficacy of their training delivery. They assessed it at several different levels of process and outcome.

> **PROCESS ASSESSMENT:**   Did the trainees give evidence of receiving the training delivery?

Given that the trainees received the training delivery, the question concerning whether they acquired the training content remained.

> **ACQUISITION ASSESSMENT:**   Did the trainees acquire the planning, producing, and assessing skills content?

Given that the trainees acquired the content, it was still necessary to inquire into their ability to apply the skills to the training objective.

> **APPLICATION ASSESSMENT:**   Did the trainees apply their skills to the planning, producing, and assessing objectives?

The more relevant question concerning the transfer of the skills to real-life tasks remained.

> **TRANSFER ASSESSMENT:**   Did the trained personnel transfer their skills to real-life consulting tasks?

Finally, the ISD personnel want to know whether they achieved their original goals.

> **ACHIEVEMENT ASSESSMENT:**   Did the trained personnel improve the quantity and quality of their individual consulting performance by 10%?

In turn, these assessments were related to the original strategic goals flowing from the internal mission.

> **STRATEGIC GOAL:**   Did the trained personnel increase their results outputs while reducing their resource inputs?

INSTRUCTIONAL EVALUATION

All of these stages of a productive intervention were developed and implemented. Upon process assessment, it was found that all of the trainees gave demonstrable evidence of receiving the training delivery: the trainees produced their own individual learning programs.

    PROCESS RESULTS: On 5-point scales, the trainees were rated at 4.7 in terms of their movement toward acting to receive the training delivery.

Acquisition assessments yielded similarly positive ratings: the trainees acquired the skill steps and knowledge of the training content.

    ACQUISITION RESULTS: On 5-point scales, the trainees were rated at 4.7 in terms of their performance of the skills.

Similarly, application assessments produced positive results: the trainees applied their skills to the training objectives simulating the real-life work tasks.

    APPLICATION RESULTS: On 5-point scales, the trainees were rated at 4.5 in terms of applying their skills to the training objectives.

Also, the assessments of transfer yielded positive results: the trained personnel transferred their skills to their consulting tasks.

    TRANSFER RESULTS: On 5-point scales, personnel were rated at 4.7 in terms of using their skills in everyday consulting tasks.

Finally, the goal achievement yielded positive results: the personnel improved their performance in consulting.

    ACHIEVEMENT RESULTS: The personnel were able to improve the quantity and quality of their performance by more than 10%.

Thus, the ISD intervention was successful in achieving its personnel performance goals. It remained to relate the ISD goals to the strategic goals and the original mission.

The success of the ISD intervention was instrumental in achieving the strategic goals.

STRATEGIC GOAL RESULTS: The organizational output increased by 25% while the resource expenditures were reduced by 16%.

Thus, by intervening with an instructional design derived systematically from its strategic goals, the IR Department was able to surpass its goals and achieve its internal mission. IR was now prepared to address its external mission, that of expanding its services throughout the entire corporation.

In summary, productive interventions begin with measurable goals derived systematically from effective policy. Where appropriate, productive interventions may end with measurable goals achieved systematically through instructional intervention. In short, instructional systems design is a vehicle for achieving desirable individual performance and organizational productivity goals through systematic intervention.

In the pages that follow, an overview of a systems approach to instructional evaluation will be presented. This introductory information on instructional evaluation is followed by a review of the steps completed when planning an evaluation. Next, an indepth coverage of the assessment levels used to evaluate instructional processes and outcomes is presented. These assessment levels form the core of a systematic evaluation. In a systematic evaluation, each instructional intervention stage corresponds to an assessment level. The basic principle of instructional evaluation is that you assess only those results your intervention was designed to affect. The outcomes must flow systematically from the instructional design or they are not outcomes--just simply random occurrences!

Work--as life--in the Age of Information--is as productive as its implementers are systematic in processing its data. For instructional technologists, processing the data inputs of the decision makers and transforming them into the performance improvements of trained personnel is part of the job.

OVERVIEW
SYSTEMS APPROACH
TO EVALUATION

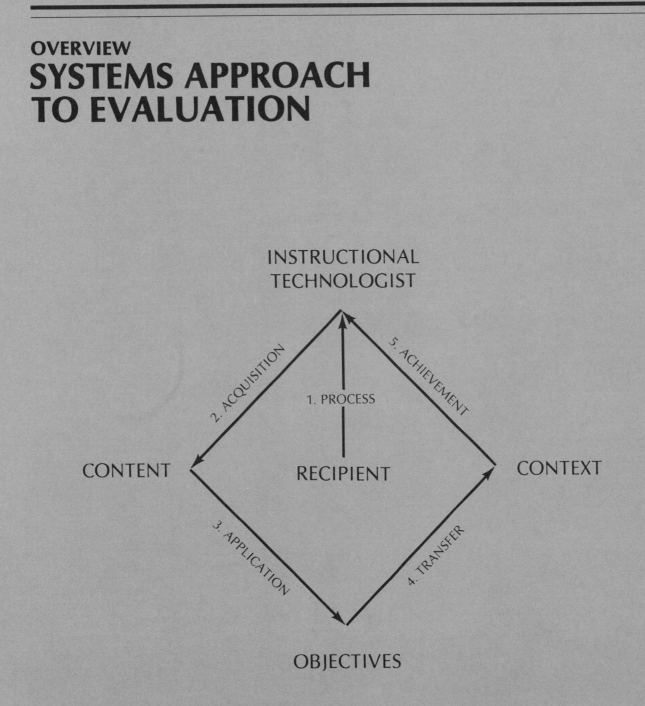

Introduction

Typically, training evaluators assess a single level of training outcome. No attention is paid to other levels of outcomes or the relationships among the various outcome levels.

For example, we may measure whether our recipients acquired the training content but fail to determine how the acquisition of that content relates to applications and transfers in the real-life context.

In a systems approach to training evaluation, we assess all levels of outcome we wish to affect. A systems approach to evaluation allows us to relate the outcomes achieved at one stage of the instructional intervention to all other stages of that intervention.

**Important
Principle**

The basic principle of instructional systems evaluation is:

> You assess only those outcomes your intervention
> was designed to affect.

A common misinterpretation of research is the idea that outcome measures must be independent of the intervention. It is correct that outcomes must be independently measured. However, the selection of outcomes to be measured must flow systematically from the instructional design. Outcomes that are not related to a systematic design are simply random occurrences.

**Instructional
Design:
    Review**

Volume I provided a detailed description of the instructional design process.

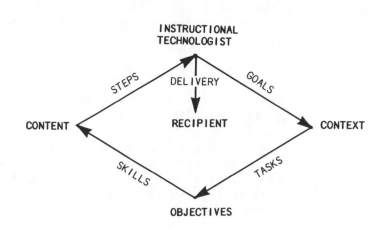

In a systematic instructional systems design, the stages of
development lead to the instructional delivery: 1) productivity goals lead to contextual tasks; 2) contextual tasks
lead to training objectives; 3) training objectives lead to
skill content; 4) skill content leads to the delivery plan;
5) the delivery plan leads to the training delivery.

**Levels Of
Assessment:
    Overview**

The levels of outcome assessment involve recycling through
the stages of the instructional intervention.

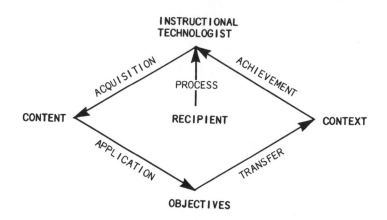

As illustrated above, the following outcome assessments are
made: 1) an assessment of the intervention process; 2) an
assessment of the recipients' acquisition of the training
content; 3) an assessment of the recipients' application of
the training content; 4) an assessment of the recipients'
transfer of the training content; 5) an assessment of productivity goal achievement.

**Relationship
Between Design
And Evaluation**

The relationship between the evaluation of instructional outcomes and the instructional design process is summarized below:

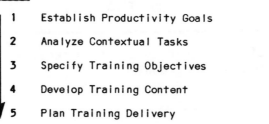

DESIGN		EVALUATION	
STAGE		LEVEL	
1	Establish Productivity Goals	5	Achievement
2	Analyze Contextual Tasks	4	Transfer
3	Specify Training Objectives	3	Application
4	Develop Training Content	2	Acquisition
5	Plan Training Delivery	1	Process

Table 1 further illustrates the relationship between the design and evaluation of instructional interventions.

**Planning The
Evaluation**

A systems approach to evaluating instructional intervention provides an overall framework for assessment. The instructional evaluator must plan how each outcome level will be evaluated. The following steps are completed when planning the evaluation of each outcome level.

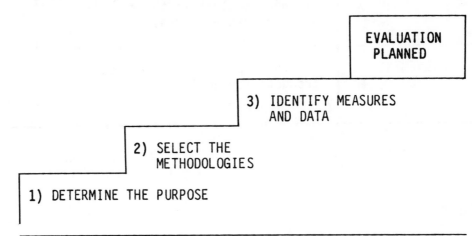

EVALUATION
PLANNED

3) IDENTIFY MEASURES
   AND DATA

2) SELECT THE
   METHODOLOGIES

1) DETERMINE THE PURPOSE

Table 1.

RELATIONSHIP BETWEEN EVALUATION AND DESIGN

ASSESSMENT LEVELS	EVALUATION QUESTION	CORRESPONDING DESIGN PHASE
PROCESS	Did the recipients act to receive the training content?	PLANNING TRAINING DELIVERY
ACQUISITION	Did the recipients acquire the training content?	DEVELOPING TRAINING CONTENT
APPLICATION	Did the recipients apply the training content to the training objective?	SPECIFYING TRAINING OBJECTIVES
TRANSFER	Did the recipients transfer the training content to their real-life contextual tasks?	ANALYZING CONTEXTUAL TASKS
ACHIEVEMENT	Did the recipients achieve the productivity goals?	ESTABLISHING PRODUCTIVITY GOALS

Relationship Between Planning Steps And Assessment Levels

The planning steps are completed for <u>each</u> assessment level. The relationship between the planning steps and assessment levels is illustrated below.

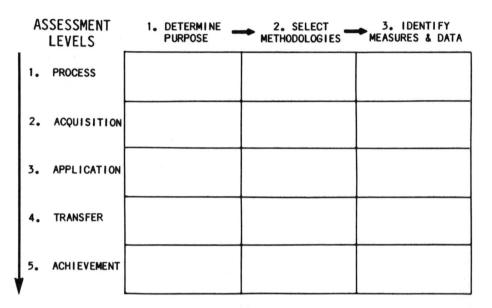

EVALUATION PLANNING STEPS

ASSESSMENT LEVELS	1. DETERMINE PURPOSE	2. SELECT METHODOLOGIES	3. IDENTIFY MEASURES & DATA
1. PROCESS			
2. ACQUISITION			
3. APPLICATION			
4. TRANSFER			
5. ACHIEVEMENT			

A systems approach to training evaluation involves planning and implementing all of the cells in the above matrix. The remainder of this volume will discuss the planning steps and the assessment levels.

Summary

The key ingredient in a systems approach to evaluation is intentionality. In the final analysis, we either achieve our goals or we do not. The instructional design process begins with the development of productivity goals. The intervention should, therefore, conclude with an assessment of goal achievement.

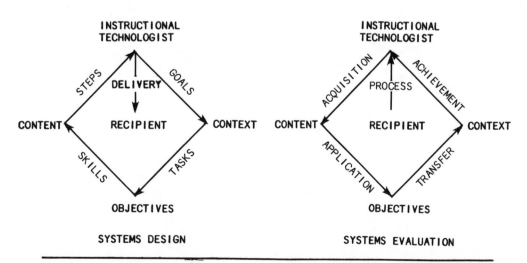

SYSTEMS DESIGN   SYSTEMS EVALUATION

PLANNING THE EVALUATION

**What Is
Planning The
Evaluation?**

Planning the evaluation involves specifying the purpose,
methodologies, measures, and types of data collected for
each level of assessment.

**Why Is Planning
Important?**

It is simply not enough to intend to assess process, acquisition, application, transfer, and achievement. We must
systematically plan how each assessment level will be evaluated.

**How Are
Evaluations
Planned?**

Planning the evaluation involves the following steps:

```
                                        ┌──────────────┐
                                        │  EVALUATION  │
                                        │   PLANNED    │
                                ┌───────┤              │
                                │ 3) IDENTIFY MEASURES │
                                │    AND DATA          │
                        ┌───────┤
                        │ 2) SELECT THE
                        │    METHODOLOGIES
                ┌───────┤
                │ 1) DETERMINE THE PURPOSE
                │
```

```
┌─────────────────────────────────────────┐
│      STEP 1:  DETERMINE THE PURPOSE      │
└─────────────────────────────────────────┘
```

What Are The Purposes Of Evaluation?

The first planning step is to identify the purpose for the assessment of each outcome level. There are two primary purposes for evaluating any training outcome:

- To JUDGE . . .

   We look at the training outcome against some criteria. This type of evaluation is referred to as SUMMATIVE EVALUATION.

- To IMPROVE . . .

   We upgrade the training outcome to meet some criteria. This type of evaluation is referred to as FORMATIVE EVALUATION.

What Is Summative Evaluation?

Summative evaluation focuses on a summary assessment of the relative success or failure of a training intervention. A summative evaluation is intended to provide decision makers with data upon which to judge the intervention and make decisions such as:

- Did we accomplish what we set out to accomplish?

- Was the outcome worth the cost?

- Should we continue, discontinue, expand, or contract the intervention?

What Is Formative Evaluation?

Formative evaluation focuses on assessing the components, processes, and functions of an ongoing training intervention. A formative evaluation provides designers and implementers with information needed to make "mid-course corrections" which will improve the effectiveness of the intervention. Formative evaluation addresses questions such as:

- Are the correct target populations involved in the intervention?

- Is the training content being delivered and received as intended?

- Are the training recipients actually accomplishing the training objectives?

PLANNING THE EVALUATION
STEP 1:   DETERMINE THE PURPOSE ▬▬▬▬▬▬▬▬▬▬▬▬▬▬▬▬▬▬▬▬

**What Is The
Traditional
Approach?**

Historically, evaluation studies were often differentiated as either process evaluations or outcome evaluations, with the accompanying assumption that process studies were formative and outcome studies were summative.

This traditional distinction between process evaluations and outcome evaluations can result in a limited data base.

**What Is The
Systems Approach?**

A broader view is that any training intervention is a complete system with inputs, processes, and outcomes.

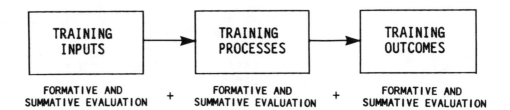

Using a systems perspective, a formative and summative evaluation may be used to assess any or all of the components of a training intervention. The distinction between formative and summative evaluation assists us in determining the _purpose_ of the evaluation. Table 2 summarizes the formative and summative purposes of training evaluation.

Table 2.

DETERMINING EVALUATION PURPOSES

PURPOSES

COMPONENTS	FORMATIVE	SUMMATIVE
TRAINING INPUTS	To determine if . . . • Resource inputs are sufficient • Changes in resource inputs are needed	To determine if . . . • Results outputs justify the resource inputs • The amount and types of future resource inputs can be specified
TRAINING PROCESSES	To determine if . . . • Processes are being implemented as planned • Adjustments in processes are required	To determine if . . . • Processes were effective • Processes should be replicated
TRAINING OUTCOMES	To determine if . . . • Short-term outcomes are being met • Short-term outcomes have implications for current training inputs or processes	To determine if . . . • Long-term outcomes were accomplished • Long-term outcomes have implications for future instructional interventions

```
┌─────────────────────────────────────────┐
│     STEP 2:   SELECT THE METHODOLOGIES   │
└─────────────────────────────────────────┘
```

What Are Evaluation Methodologies?

The next step is to select the evaluation methodologies. The major dimensions of evaluation methodologies are illustrated below:

EVALUATION METHODOLOGIES

EXPERIMENTAL

```
                    ↑
                    │
                    │
STATIC ←────────────┼────────────→ DYNAMIC
                    │
                    │
                    ↓
```

NATURALISTIC

Think of this figure as a graph. The two dimensions are continual, and any given evaluation design can be plotted somewhere on the graph.

Static vs. Dynamic

The static vs. dynamic dimension refers to the frequency of the data collection. Designs that call for a one-time data collection effort are considered static evaluations. Continuous data collection efforts are considered dynamic.

Experimental vs. Naturalistic

The experimental vs. naturalistic dimension relates to the degree to which the design involves experimental controls and manipulations. A further explanation of experimental and naturalistic design concepts is presented on the following pages.

**What Are
Experimental
Designs?**

EXPERIMENTAL evaluation designs maximize the control an evaluator has over the variables and conditions in a study. The control reduces the intrusion of the unexpected factors and increases the evaluator's confidence in the interpretation of the study's results.

The disadvantages of highly-controlled experimental designs are summarized below:

- The implementation of experimental designs may be difficult and costly.

- The results obtained may not apply (or be generalizable) to real-life situations.

**Example:
    Experimental
    Design**

A famous example of the limitations of experimental designs comes from a series of studies in psychology.

Evaluators, using highly-controlled experimental procedures, established several laws of learning by experimenting with the behavior of laboratory rats running through mazes to reach a food reward.

Unfortunately, the laws did not even generalize to other rats, let alone to humans. When city dump rats were studied, they did not even try to run through the maze. The city rats simply chewed through the walls of the maze and grabbed the food.

**What Are
Naturalistic
Designs?**

NATURALISTIC evaluation designs maximize the "true-to-life" conditions under which something is being studied. If results occur, and continually reoccur, in naturalistic studies, an evaluator can feel relatively confident that a "real-life" effect is occurring.

The disadvantages of naturalistic designs are summarized below:

- It is often difficult to know what variables are really causing the effects.

- Conducting the evaluation, itself, may change the conditions so that they are no longer "true-to-life" or naturalistic.

Example:
Naturalistic
Design

An example from applied social science research, the famous "Hawthorne Effect" studies, clearly demonstrated the limitations of naturalistic studies.

After initial studies, researchers concluded that worker productivity was increased when better lighting was provided in a work area.

Later studies showed that putting workers in poorer lighting also increased worker productivity.

Finally, it was concluded that increased worker productivity was simply a result of the attention being paid to the workers and their work area rather than an effect of the brightness of the lighting.

The real learning here was that, without extensive experimental controls, it is very difficult to be sure which causes are clearly related to which outcomes.

What Are
Constant
Feedback
Systems?

The logical extension of the trend toward dynamic evaluations is that evaluation will cease to be viewed as a separate activity. Constant feedback systems will be designed and implemented as an integral part of most training interventions.

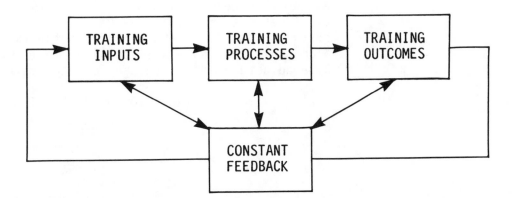

Constant feedback systems allow designers and implementers to access changing formative data on a daily, hourly, or moment-by-moment basis.

The constant feedback will enable decision makers to review changing summative data at any time, with impact data (including costs and benefits) being kept current right up to the point in time that crucial decisions must be made.

What Is The Traditional Approach?

Most traditional evaluations have been static. That is, whether the purpose was formative or summative, evaluators picked a point in time to "draw a line and collect data."

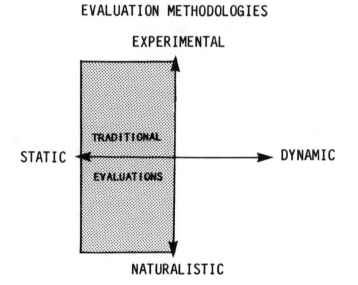

EVALUATION METHODOLOGIES

EXPERIMENTAL

STATIC ←————— TRADITIONAL EVALUATIONS —————→ DYNAMIC

NATURALISTIC

What Is The Systems Approach?

As we move into the Age of Information, with daily changes in information and communication technology, it will become increasingly possible and practical to implement dynamic evaluation designs. However, a systems approach to evaluation does not impact an evaluator's design decisions on the experimental vs. naturalistic continuum. Design decisions along this continuum will still be made based on the relative advantages/disadvantages of each methodology.

EVALUATION METHODOLOGIES

EXPERIMENTAL

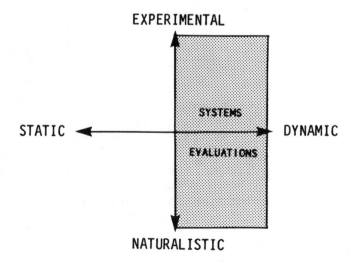

STATIC ←————— SYSTEMS EVALUATIONS —————→ DYNAMIC

NATURALISTIC

STEP 3:   IDENTIFY MEASURES AND DATA

What Are Types Of Measures And Data?

The third design step is to identify the types of measures and data to be collected. The major types of evaluation measures and data are:

TYPES OF DATA

TYPES OF MEASURES	OBJECTIVE	SUBJECTIVE
CRITERION-REFERENCED		
NORM-REFERENCED		

What Are Criterion-Referenced Measures?

The most basic characteristic of a criterion-referenced measure is that a TARGET or STANDARD of performance is established:

- **Before** the measure is constructed
                     - and -
- **Before** the trainee or program is tested.

**Purpose:
    Criterion-Referenced Measures**

The purpose of criterion-referenced measures is to establish how each trainee or program performs in relation to a preset criterion.

There is only <u>one</u> question that is addressed by criterion-referenced measures:

"Did the trainee or program achieve the criterion or not?"

There are only two possible answers to the criterion-referenced measure question: "Yes" or "No."

Criterion-referenced measures are <u>not</u> intended to provide information about how different trainees or programs compare with each other.

Uses:
    Criterion-
    Referenced
    Measures

Criterion-referenced measures are used when:

- The goals or performance objectives of instruction have been clearly specified and operationalized.

- The focus of interest is on the achievement of a specified standard of performance rather than on the relative standings among several individuals, groups, or programs.

What Are Norm-
Referenced
Measures?

The most basic characteristic of a norm-referenced measure is that the assessment information generated is about <u>relative</u> performance of individuals, groups, or programs.

Purpose:
    Norm-Referenced
    Measures

The purpose of norm-referenced measures is to provide discriminations or distinctions among individuals, groups, or programs.

Many questions are addressed by norm-referenced measures. Examples of questions addressed by norm-referenced measures include:

"How did Individual X perform in relation to the average score on this measure?"

"How did men and women differ on these measures?"

"Who were the top ten performers in this area?"

"How did the trainees in this course compare with the last group of trainees who took this course?"

"How did the outcome of Program X compare with the outcome of Program Y?"

Uses:
    Norm-Referenced
    Measures

Norm-referenced measures are used when:

- A decision must be made based on comparisons among individuals, groups, or programs.

- The focus of interest is on the range of performance in a given area rather than on the achievement of a prespecified standard of performance.

What Are Objective Data?

Objective data have three primary characteristics. They are:

- **OBSERVABLE:** Observable data can be seen or sensed by humans or by instruments created by humans.

- **MEASURABLE:** Measurable data can be assigned a label or number that distinguishes one piece of data from another piece of data.

- **VERIFIABLE:** Verifiable data can be observed and measured by more than one person.

What Are Subjective Data?

Subjective data are values, attitudes, feelings, and opinions of one or more persons. These data do not have the three characteristics of objective data. However, subjective data may be equally (or more) important than objective data in the evaluation of any particular training outcome.

Can Subjective Data Be Objectified?

The development of methods to objectify or operationalize subjective experience has been an important contribution to educational and social science education.

Using an interpersonal interaction process, evaluators have worked with a variety of people to help them specify values, attitudes, feelings, and opinions in a way that is observable, measurable and verifiable.

The method that is used in this process is called Favorability Scaling.

This method is important enough to the instructional evaluator that we will present it in some detail in a later section of this volume.

What Is The Traditional Approach?

The traditional evaluation approach in training is to use norm-referenced measures of subjective data.

TYPES OF DATA

TYPES OF MEASURES	OBJECTIVE	SUBJECTIVE
CRITERION-REFERENCED		
NORM-REFERENCED		TRADITIONAL EVALUATION

For example, the percentage of trainees who rate the training experience as satisfactory is a norm-referenced measure of subjective data.

What Is The Systems Approach?

The systems approach to training evaluation is to select the types of measures and data based on the questions to be answered by the formative and summative purposes of the evaluation.

TYPES OF DATA

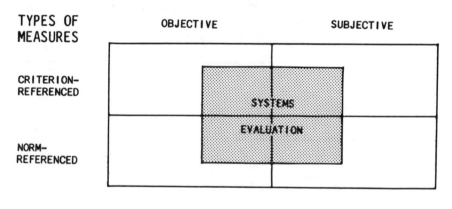

TYPES OF MEASURES	OBJECTIVE	SUBJECTIVE
CRITERION-REFERENCED	SYSTEMS	
NORM-REFERENCED	EVALUATION	

Planning Steps And Assessment Levels

Remember, the evaluation planning steps are completed for all levels of assessments.

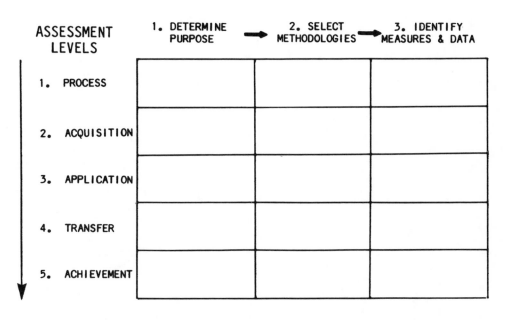

EVALUATION PLANNING STEPS

ASSESSMENT LEVELS	1. DETERMINE PURPOSE	2. SELECT METHODOLOGIES	3. IDENTIFY MEASURES & DATA
1. PROCESS			
2. ACQUISITION			
3. APPLICATION			
4. TRANSFER			
5. ACHIEVEMENT			

Key Planning Concepts

Following are the key concepts to keep in mind when completing each planning step.

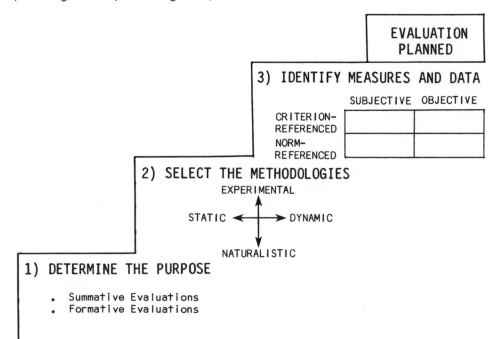

EVALUATION PLANNED

3) IDENTIFY MEASURES AND DATA

	SUBJECTIVE	OBJECTIVE
CRITERION-REFERENCED		
NORM-REFERENCED		

2) SELECT THE METHODOLOGIES

EXPERIMENTAL

STATIC ←→ DYNAMIC

NATURALISTIC

1) DETERMINE THE PURPOSE

- Summative Evaluations
- Formative Evaluations

31

ASSESSMENT LEVELS

**What Are
Assessment
Levels?**

As noted earlier, a systems approach to training evaluation measures all outcomes that your intervention was designed to affect. Following are the assessment levels evaluated:

ASSESSMENT LEVELS

5	GOAL ACHIEVEMENT	Did the recipients achieve the productivity goals?
4	TASK TRANSFER	Did the recipients transfer the training content to their real-life contextual tasks?
3	SKILL APPLICATION	Did the recipients apply the training content to the training objectives?
2	CONTENT ACQUISITION	Did the recipients acquire the training content?
1	PROCESS MOVEMENT	Did the recipients act to receive the training content?

A detailed description of these assessment levels will be presented following this overview.

**How Do The
Assessment
Levels
Interact?**

In a systemic instructional design, each stage builds on the one that preceded it. For example, if we fail to analyze the contextual tasks, we are unable to specify training objectives that will respond to the requirements of the real-life context.

Similarly, the outcome achieved at each level relates to every subsequent level of outcome. While each outcome level is necessary, a single outcome is not sufficient for the achievement of the next level. For example, successful content acquisition will not automatically lead to successful skill applications. On the other hand, failure to acquire content will preclude skill applications.

Figure 1 illustrates the interactions among the assessment levels.

Figure 1.

INTERACTIONS AMONG ASSESSMENT LEVELS

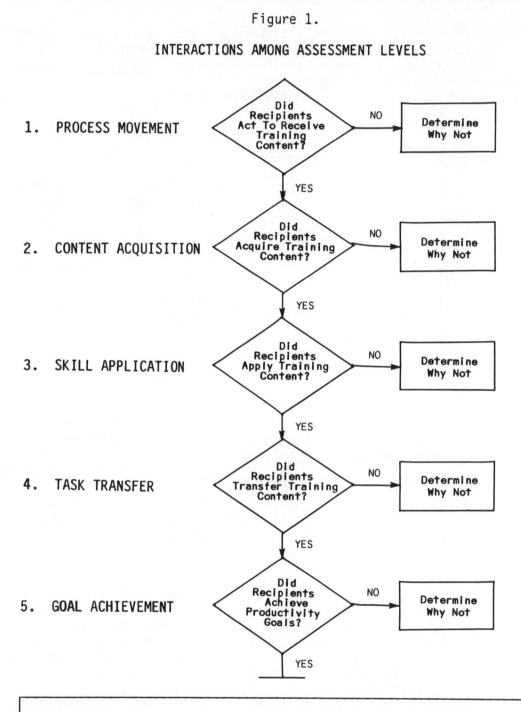

1. PROCESS MOVEMENT

2. CONTENT ACQUISITION

3. SKILL APPLICATION

4. TASK TRANSFER

5. GOAL ACHIEVEMENT

EXPLANATION: Your evaluation should end if you reach a "no" answer at any assessment level. For example, if the recipients did not transfer the skill to their work setting, then we can predict that our productivity goal cannot be achieved. It would be inefficient to continue the evaluation.

ASSESSING PROCESS MOVEMENT

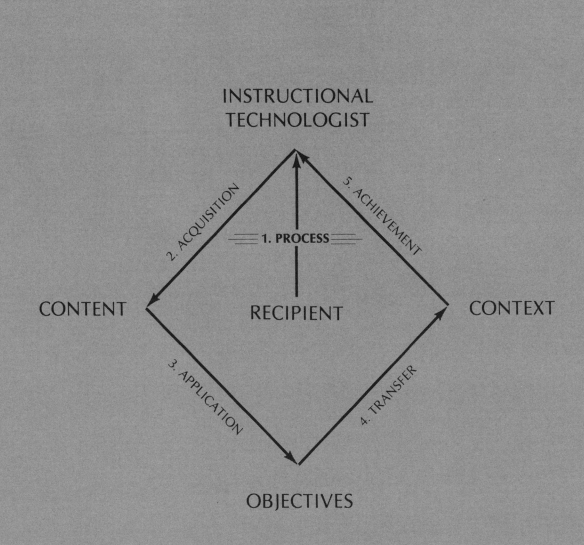

What Is Assessing Process Movement?

The essential task in assessing training process is to measure the recipients' movement in receiving the training content. The process assessment answers the question: Did the recipients act to receive the training content?

What Are Recipient Processes?

An illustration reviewing the processes recipients engage in in order to receive the training content is presented below.

RECIPIENT PROCESSES

Involving ⟶ Exploring ⟶ Understanding ⟶ Acting

What Is Involving?

Involving is the most fundamental level of recipient processes. Involving simply means that the recipients physically attended, observed, listened to, and participated in the training.

RECIPIENT PROCESSES

Involving

What Is Exploring?

Exploring is the process used by recipients to identify their entry performance levels. Exploration allows the recipients to know precisely where they are in relation to the training experience.

RECIPIENT PROCESSES

Involving ⟶ Exploring

"Where They Are"

What Is Understanding?

Understanding is the process used by recipients to establish their own personal learning goals. In terms of the training process, recipients must understand where they are in relation to where they want to be.

RECIPIENT PROCESSES

Involving ⟶ Exploring ⟶ Understanding

"Where They Are"   "Where They Want To Be"

What Is Acting?   Acting is the process used by recipients in order to achieve their personal learning goals. Recipients act to develop their own individualized learning programs.

RECIPIENT PROCESSES

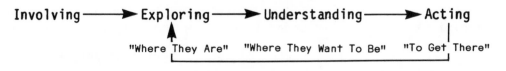

How Is Process
Movement
Measured?

Recipient process movement can be measured using a developmental scale. A developmental scale is a form of favorability scaling (see the Appendix of this volume for a description of scaling techniques).

PROCESS MOVEMENT SCALE

LEVELS

5	ACTING	Did the recipients act to achieve their learning goals?
4	UNDERSTANDING	Did the recipients establish an understanding of their learning goals?
3	EXPLORING	Did the recipients explore where they were in relation to the training experience?
2	INVOLVING	Did the recipients become involved in the training process by attending, observing, and listening?
1	NON-INVOLVING	Did the recipients fail to become involved in the training?

Table 3 provides a further explanation of the process movement scale.

40

Table 3.

UNDERSTANDING THE PROCESS MOVEMENT SCALE

	LEVELS	EXPLANATION
5	ACTING	At Level 5, recipients: • <u>Act</u> to implement their learning programs • <u>Understand</u> and set individualized learning goals • <u>Explore</u> themselves in relation to the content • <u>Involve</u> themselves in the training experience
4	UNDERSTANDING	At Level 4, recipients: • Do not act to implement their learning programs • <u>Understand</u> and set individualized learning goals • <u>Explore</u> themselves in relation to the content • <u>Involve</u> themselves in the training experience
3	EXPLORING	At Level 3, recipients: • Do not act to implement their learning programs • Do not understand and set individualized learning goals • <u>Explore</u> themselves in relation to the content • <u>Involve</u> themselves in the training experience
2	INVOLVING	At Level 2, recipients: • Do not act to implement their learning programs • Do not understand and set individualized learning goals • Do not explore themselves in relation to the content • <u>Involve</u> themselves in the training experience
1	NON-INVOLVING	At Level 1, recipients: • Do not act to implement their learning programs • Do not understand and set individualized learning goals • Do not explore themselves in relation to the content • Do not involve themselves in the training experience

What Are The Process Indices?

The following behavioral indices may be used to assist us in discriminating the levels of recipient process movement.

PROCESS MOVEMENT SCALE

LEVELS		INDICES
5	ACTING	. Implementing Learning Programs . Individualizing Learning Programs . Developing Learning Programs
4	UNDERSTANDING	. Defining Individual Goals . Personalizing Individual Goals . Setting Individual Goals
3	EXPLORING	. Determining One's Own Entry Level . Diagnosing Selves . Analyzing Training Content
2	INVOLVING	. Listening . Observing . Attending Physically
1	NON-INVOLVING	. Not Listening . Not Observing . Not Attending

Can A Process Criterion Be Established?

A criterion is built into the process movement scale. The criterion for recipient process movement is LEVEL 5: ACTING. If recipients fail to act, then it follows that recipients will be unable to acquire the training content. The remaining levels of the process movement scale are used to assess the extent of the recipient involvement.

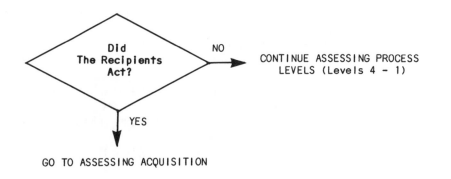

Did The Recipients Act?

NO → CONTINUE ASSESSING PROCESS LEVELS (Levels 4 - 1)

YES → GO TO ASSESSING ACQUISITION

Are There Other Ways To Assess Process?

Traditionally, training processes are assessed using norm-referenced measures of subjective data. Following are example items designed to measure recipients' attitudes concerning their process movement:

SAMPLE SUBJECTIVE RATINGS

ITEMS	RATINGS
1. I found the training:	1 2 3 4 5 → Boring Exciting
2. The training content was:	1 2 3 4 5 → Irrelevant Very Relevant
3. My learning goals were:	1 2 3 4 5 → Not Addressed Fully Addressed
4. Overall, I felt the training process was:	1 2 3 4 5 → Less Than Satisfactory More Than Satisfactory

What Implications Can Be Derived From Process Data?

Data derived from an assessment of recipient process movement have implications for instructional design and delivery personnel. If training recipients fail to act to receive the training content, then we must look for weaknesses in the training delivery process. The training delivery process involves:

- Content Processing Skills

- Interpersonal Processing Skills

A brief explanation of these training delivery skills follows. Individuals seeking additional information should review **Training Delivery Skills, Volume II** by Carkhuff and Pierce.

What Are Content Processing Skills?

Content processing skills (CPS) are the skills employed by the trainer to facilitate recipient process movement in relation to the training content. The relationship between recipient process movement and a trainer's content processing skills is illustrated below:

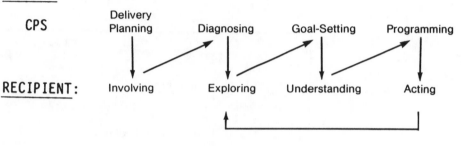

What Are Interpersonal Processing Skills?

Interpersonal processing skills (IPS) are the skills employed by the trainer to relate the training content to the recipients' experiences. The relationship between recipient process movement and trainer's delivery skills (CPS and IPS) is illustrated below:

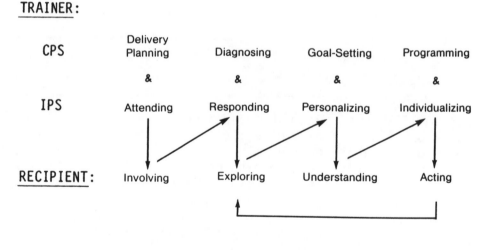

How Can The Ratings Be Used?

We can use the assessment data collected to explore, understand, and act on our own strengths and weaknesses as instructional designers and delivery personnel. The following table summarizes the relationship between the rating level achieved and the potential deficits in a trainer's delivery skills.

RATING LEVEL ACHIEVED	TRAINER SKILL DEFICIT	
	CPS	IPS
5 ACTING	. None	. None
4 UNDERSTANDING	. Programming	. Individualizing
3 EXPLORING	. Programming . Goal-Setting	. Individualizing . Personalizing
2 INVOLVING	. Programming . Goal-Setting . Diagnosing	. Individualizing . Personalizing . Responding
1 NON-INVOLVING	. Programming . Goal-Setting . Diagnosing . Delivery Planning	. Individualizing . Personalizing . Responding . Attending

Summary

However you choose to measure recipient process movement, the essential question to be answered is: Did the recipients act to receive the training content?

In planning your assessment of recipient process movement, remember to complete the following planning steps.

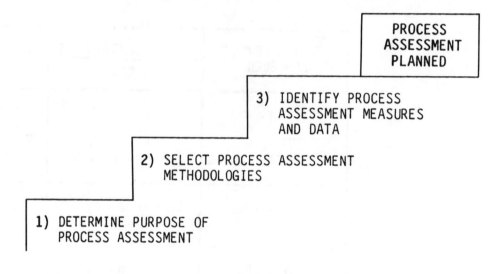

```
                                            ┌──────────────┐
                                            │   PROCESS    │
                                            │  ASSESSMENT  │
                                            │   PLANNED    │
                                            └──────────────┘
                              3) IDENTIFY PROCESS
                                 ASSESSMENT MEASURES
                                 AND DATA
                 2) SELECT PROCESS ASSESSMENT
                    METHODOLOGIES
    1) DETERMINE PURPOSE OF
       PROCESS ASSESSMENT
```

- PLANNING JOB AID -

STEP 1: DETERMINE THE PURPOSE

- The purpose of the process
  assessment is: ☐ Summative ☐ Formative

STEP 2: SELECT THE METHODOLOGIES

- The evaluation design will be: ☐ Experimental ☐ Naturalistic

- Data collection will be: ☐ Static: Indicate When _____
  ☐ Dynamic: Indicate When _____

STEP 3: IDENTIFY MEASURES AND DATA

- The types of measures to be used ☐ Criterion-Referenced
  are: ☐ Norm-Referenced

- The types of data to be collected are: ☐ Objective ☐ Subjective

- Will a favorability scale be used? ☐ Yes ☐ No

  IF YES . . . Construct your process assessment scale.

  LEVELS   **INDICES**

5

4

3

2

1

ASSESSING CONTENT ACQUISITION

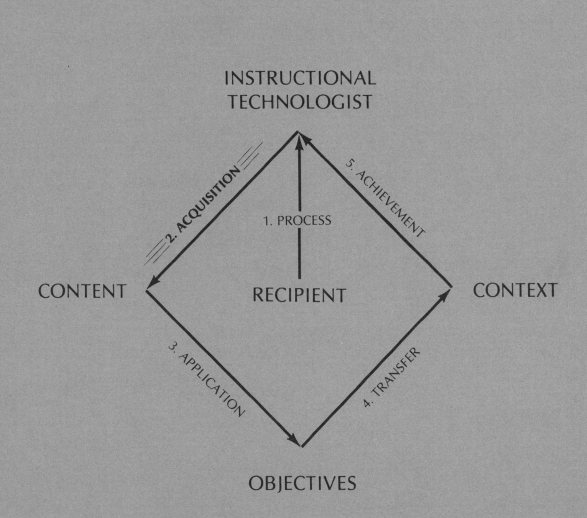

**What Is
Assessing
Content
Acquisition?**

The essential task in assessing content acquisition is to determine the level of skills and knowledge possessed by the recipients. The acquisition assessment answers the question: Did the recipients acquire the training content?

**What Is
Training
Content?**

Training content is made up of the skills, steps, and supportive knowledge. The relationships among the training content components are illustrated below.

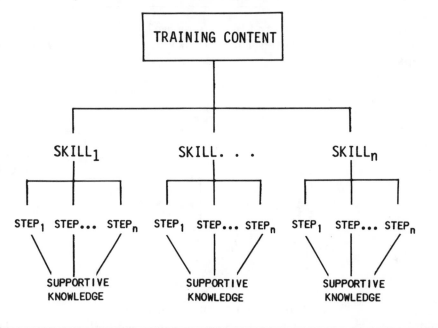

**What Are
Skills?**

Skills are those behaviors which, when added together, will lead to the accomplishment of the training objective. During the design phase, we identified skills by asking: What behaviors will lead to the accomplishment of this training objective?

**Example:
   Identifying
   Skills**

The following example illustrates how skills are identified:

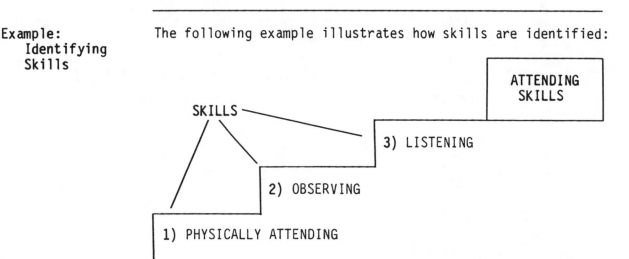

What Are Steps?   Steps are those sub-behaviors which, when added together, will lead to the performance of the skill. Each skill is broken down into small, sequenced steps that the recipients must do in order to perform the skill. The skill steps must be broken down into units that the recipients can successfully learn, practice, and master. During the design phase we identified skill steps by asking: How do the recipients do the skill?

**Example:
  Identifying
  Steps**

The following example illustrates how skill steps are identified for the skill of physically attending.

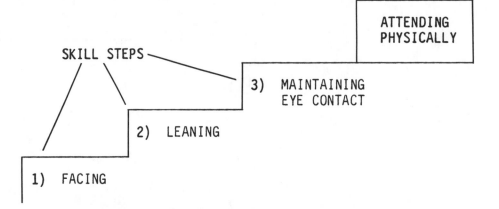

**What Is
Supportive
Knowledge?**

Supportive knowledge includes those facts, concepts, and principles which are needed in order to perform a skill or skill step.

SUPPORTIVE KNOWLEDGE

FACTS: Facts name the components, functions, and processes of a skill or training objective.

CONCEPTS: Concepts describe how the various facts affect one another.

               "If (cause) , then (effect) ."

PRINCIPLES: Principles organize the facts and concepts around their implications.

               "If (cause) , then (effect) , so that   (implication) ."

Example:
Identifying
Supportive
Knowledge

The following example presents the knowledge (facts, concepts, and principles) that supports the performance of the attending skills:

SUPPORTIVE KNOWLEDGE

PRINCIPLES: If the trainer uses attending skills when delivering training content, then the recipient process movement will be facilitated so that the training content can be acquired.

CONCEPTS: If the trainer attends to the recipients, then the recipients are more likely to become involved in the training process.

FACTS: Trainer, recipients, physically attending, observing, and listening.

How Is Content
Acquisition
Measured?

Recipient content acquisition can be measured using a developmental scale. Remember, a developmental scale is a form of favorability scaling (see the Appendix of this volume for a description of scaling techniques).

CONTENT ACQUISITION SCALE

LEVELS

5	SKILLS	Did the recipients perform the skills?
4	STEPS	Did the recipients perform the skill steps?
3	PRINCIPLES	Did the recipients acquire all of the principles?
2	CONCEPTS	Did the recipients acquire all of the conceptual knowledge?
1	FACTS	Did the recipients acquire all of the factual knowledge?

Table 4 provides a further explanation of the content acquisition scale.

Table 4.

UNDERSTANDING THE CONTENT ACQUISITION SCALE

LEVELS	EXPLANATION
5 SKILLS	At Level 5, recipients: • Perform the skill • Perform the skill steps • Understand the principles • Understand the concepts • Understand the facts
4 STEPS	At Level 4, recipients: • Cannot integrate the skill steps in order to perform the skills • Perform the skill steps • Understand the principles • Understand the concepts • Understand the facts
3 PRINCIPLES	At Level 3, recipients: • Cannot perform the skills • Cannot perform the skill steps • Understand the principles • Understand the concepts • Understand the facts
2 CONCEPTS	At Level 2, recipients: • Cannot perform the skills • Cannot perform the skill steps • Do not understand the principles • Understand the concepts • Understand the facts
1 FACTS	At Level 1, recipients: • Cannot perform the skills • Cannot perform the skill steps • Do not understand the principles • Do not understand the concepts • Understand the facts

What Are The Content Acquisition Indices?

Behavioral indices may be developed for each content acquisition assessment level. Table 5 presents sample indices for assessing content acquisition.

Can An Acquisition Criterion Be Established?

A criterion is built into the content acquisition scale. The criterion for recipient content acquisition is LEVEL 5: SKILLS. If the recipients fail to perform the skills, then it follows that recipients will be unable to apply the training content. The remaining levels of the content acquisition scale can be used to assess the extent of the recipients' mastery of the content.

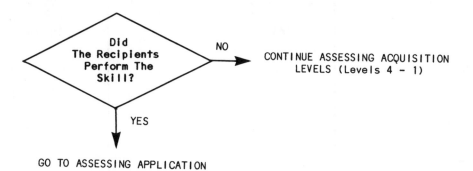

Are There Other Ways To Assess Acquisition?

Content acquisition may also be assessed using norm-referenced measures of recipients' attitudes concerning their level of content acquisition. The following sample items are designed to measure recipients' attitudes toward their acquisition of the training content:

SAMPLE SUBJECTIVE RATINGS

SKILLS	I Don't Understand The Skill		I Understand, But Don't Feel I Can Do The Skill		I Understand, And Feel I Can Do The Skill Well
Physically Attending	1	2	3	4	5
Observing	1	2	3	4	5
Listening	1	2	3	4	5

Table 5.

DEVELOPING CONTENT ACQUISITION INDICES

	LEVELS	INDICES	EXAMPLES
5	SKILLS	• Recipients can perform the skill using all of the appropriate processes or methods.	• Recipients demonstrated their planning skills by using the MBO method of planning.
4	STEPS	• Recipients can perform all of the required skill steps.	• Recipients performed the steps of planning including: 1) defining roles and missions, 2) determining key result areas, 3) specifying indicators of effectiveness, 4) selecting and setting objectives, 5) preparing action plans.
3	PRINCIPLES	• Recipients can demonstrate their understanding of principles.	• Recipients stated the principles of planning using the following format: If (cause) , then (effect) , so that (implication).
2	CONCEPTS	• Recipients can demonstrate their conceptual understanding.	• Recipients stated the planning concepts using the following format: If (cause) , then (effect) .
1	FACTS	• Recipients can demonstrate their factual understanding.	• Recipients labeled all relevant planning facts.

**How Are
Acquistion
Data Used
During
Training
Delivery?**

Content acquisition data generated during a training session can be used by training delivery personnel to make adjustments in the training delivery. For example, if a trainer diagnoses a skill performance deficit, then that trainer assesses the recipients' levels of skill step performance and supportive knowledge. The following figure illustrates how acquisition data can be used to make "mid-course" adjustments during a training delivery.

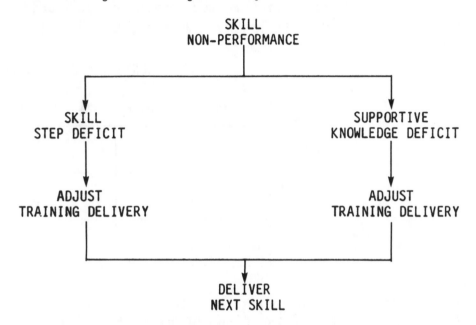

**How Are
Acquisition
Data Used
During
Instructional
Design?**

Content acquisition data can be used to modify existing instructional designs. If training recipients fail to acquire the training content, then we must look for weaknesses in our:

- Training Delivery Plan

- Training Content Development

A brief explanation of these instructional design skills follows. Individuals seeking additional information about these skills should review Volume I of this series.

Using Acquisition Data To Improve Training Delivery Plans

The training delivery plan organizes the content and establishes the methods to be used when making the delivery.

The training content is organized to include the following: reviewing the recipients' entry-level skills, overviewing the skill applications, presenting and exercising the skill steps, and summarizing the recipients' skill performance.

The training methods are organized around a variety of media for telling, showing, and doing the skills.

CONTENT ORGANIZATION

TRAINING METHODS	REVIEW	OVERVIEW	PRESENT	EXERCISE	SUMMARY
TELL					
SHOW					
DO					

If recipients fail to acquire the training content, we must ask if our plan addressed all of the cells in the above matrix.

Using Acquisition Data To Improve Content Development

Training content development is the process used to identify the skills, skill steps, and supportive knowledge.

If the recipients fail to achieve the training content, then we ask . . .

CONTENT	REVIEW QUESTIONS
SKILLS	• Do your skills lead to the achievement of the training objective?
STEPS	• Do the steps, when added together, lead to the performance of the skill? • Is the first step so simple as to seem absurd?
SUPPORTIVE KNOWLEDGE	• Will recipients have the facts, concepts, and principles needed to support the performance of the skills?

Summary

However you choose to measure recipient content acquisition, the essential question to be answered is: Did the recipients acquire the training content?

In planning your assessment of recipient content acquisition, remember to complete the following planning steps.

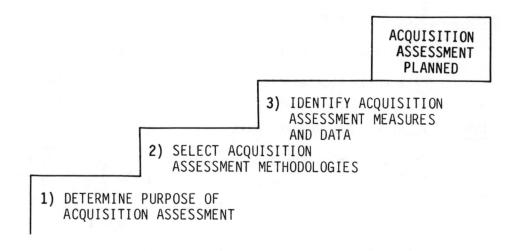

ACQUISITION
ASSESSMENT
PLANNED

3) IDENTIFY ACQUISITION
ASSESSMENT MEASURES
AND DATA

2) SELECT ACQUISITION
ASSESSMENT METHODOLOGIES

1) DETERMINE PURPOSE OF
ACQUISITION ASSESSMENT

- PLANNING JOB AID -

STEP 1: DETERMINE THE PURPOSE

- The purpose of the acquisition
  assessment is: ☐ Summative   ☐ Formative

STEP 2: SELECT THE METHODOLOGIES

- The evaluation design will be: ☐ Experimental   ☐ Naturalistic

- Data collection will be: ☐ Static: Indicate When _____
                                        ☐ Dynamic: Indicate When _____

STEP 3: IDENTIFY MEASURES AND DATA

- The types of measures to be used   ☐ Criterion-Referenced
  are: ☐ Norm-Referenced

- The types of data to be collect-
  ed are: ☐ Objective   ☐ Subjective

- Will a favorability scale be used? ☐ Yes   ☐ No

  IF YES . . . Construct your acquisition assessment scale.

  LEVELS   INDICES

5

4

3

2

1

ASSESSING SKILL APPLICATION

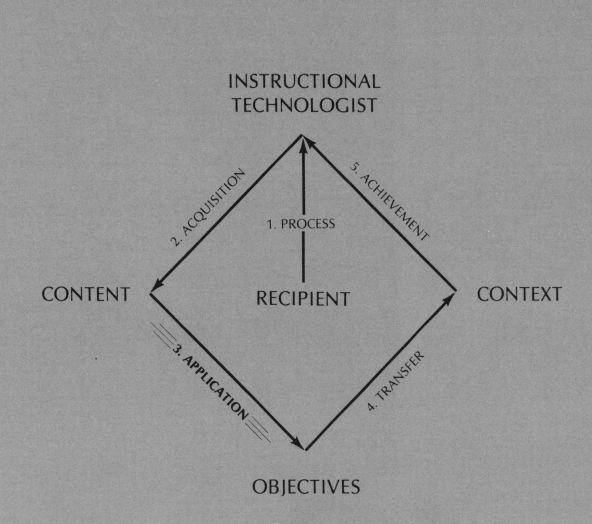

What Is Assessing Skill Application?

The essential task in assessing skill application is to determine if the recipients applied their skills to the achievement of the training objectives. The application assessment answers the question: Did the recipients apply the training content to the dimensions of the training objective?

How Does Acquisition Differ From Application?

A very important distinction must be made between the assessment of content acquisition and skill application. Our assessment of content acquisition told us whether or not the recipients performed the skill. An assessment of application goes one step further. We now determine if the skill was performed in a manner that meets the training objective.

TYPE OF ASSESSMENT	TELLS US . . .
Acquisition	Whether or not recipients performed the skills.
Application	Whether or not recipients performed the skills . . .

√ At the desired level of excellence

√ Under the prescribed conditions

√ Using the correct methods

√ To achieve the desired functions or outcomes

√ Using all the basic ingredients

Training objectives are a critical component of an application assessment. We will briefly review the development of training objectives prior to discussing application assessments.

**What Are The
Dimensions Of
An Objective?**

The dimensions of a training objective are as follows:

COMPONENTS:	Who and what things are involved?
FUNCTIONS:	What will be done?
PROCESSES:	How will it be done?
CONDITIONS:	Where, when, and why will it be done?
STANDARDS:	How well will it be done?

**What Are
Components?**

The components of a training objective are always nouns describing persons, data, or things involved in performing the skill or task. The most important component in any training objective is the training recipient. Sometimes components also include other things such as tools, special materials, machinery, or computers.

**Example:
  Components**

The following example illustrates how components are defined:

Components: Given the productivity goals and data from the contextual analysis, the ISD trainees . . .

**What Are
Functions?**

The functions of a training objective describe the desired behaviors to be performed by the training recipients. The functions are always verbs describing the desired behavioral outcomes of the training intervention.

**Example:
  Functions**

The following example illustrates how functions are defined:

Components: Given the productivity goals and data from
                the contextual analysis, the ISD trainees
Functions: will specify training objectives . . .

**What Are
Processes?**

Processes are the means by which the functions are performed. The processes are adverbs that modify the functions of the training objective. Often, the processes are a straight-forward account of the activities necessary to achieve the desired behavioral outcome. Sometimes special methods or alternative procedures are included in the processes.

**Example:
  Processes**

The following example illustrates how processes are defined:

Components:	Given the productivity goals and data from the contextual analysis, the ISD trainees
Functions:	will specify training objectives
Processes:	by defining components, functions, processes, conditions, and standards . . .

**What Are
Conditions?**

Conditions are adverbial phrases that tell us:

- **Where:** The "where" tells us the context in which the functions and processes take place. Understanding the context is important as the training recipients start to transfer their learnings from the training environment to other environments such as the work setting.

- **When:** The "when" tells us the beginning and end of the timeline for performing the objective. Timelines also tell us when to observe or measure the behavior to determine if the objective has been achieved.

**Example:
  Conditions**

The following example illustrates how conditions are defined:

Components:	Given the productivity goals and data from the contextual analysis, the ISD trainees
Functions:	will specify training objectives
Processes:	by defining components, functions, processes, conditions, and standards
Conditions:	after conducting a contextual analysis and before establishing training content so that training objectives relate to productivity goals . . .

**What Are
Standards?**

Standards are adverbial phrases that describe the desired level of excellence to be achieved. Standards may be absolute or relative.

**Example:
   Standards**

The following example illustrates how standards are defined:

Components:	Given the productivity goals and data from the contextual analysis, the ISD trainees
Functions:	will specify training objectives
Processes:	by defining components, functions, processes, conditions, and standards
Conditions:	after conducting a contextual analysis and before establishing training content so that training objectives relate to productivity goals
Standards:	at a 90% level of accuracy as measured by a master trainer.

**How Is Skill
Application
Measured?**

Skill application can be measured using a developmental scale to rate recipient performance in a simulation. As noted earlier, a developmental scale is a form of favorability scaling (see the Appendix of this volume for a description of scaling techniques).

SKILL APPLICATION SCALE

LEVELS

5	STANDARDS	Did the recipients apply their skills at the prescribed standards?
4	CONDITIONS	Did the recipients apply their skills under the prescribed conditions?
3	PROCESSES	Did the recipients apply their skills using the prescribed methods?
2	FUNCTIONS	Did the recipients apply their skills to the activities or purposes?
1	COMPONENTS	Did the recipients apply their skills using the basic ingredients?

Continued . . .

How Is Skill Application Measured? (Continued)

Table 6 presents a further explanation of the skill application scale.

NOTE: Conditions play an important role in assessing skill application. It is, therefore, extremely important that the simulation used to rate application reflect both the stated and implied conditions under which recipients will be expected to perform the training objectives.

What Are The Skill Application Indices?

Behavioral indices for skill application should already exist. A well-constructed training objective will include behavioral indices. You may want to expand or clarify these indices before assessing skill application. Table 7 provides a list of questions that may help you to develop your application indices.

Can An Application Criterion Be Established?

A criterion is built into the skill application scale. The criterion for recipient application is LEVEL 5: STANDARDS. Remember, the application scale is developmental or cumulative. This means that . . .

LEVEL 5 = SKILL PERFORMANCE

√ At prescribed standards

√ Under prescribed conditions

√ Using correct processes

√ To achieve desired functions

√ Using all components

If the recipients fail to reach the standard of excellence prescribed by the training objectives, then it follows that recipients will not be able to fully transfer their skills to performing their contextual tasks.

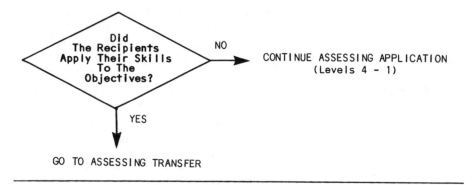

Table 6.

UNDERSTANDING THE SKILL APPLICATION SCALE

LEVELS	EXPLANATION
5 STANDARDS	At Level 5, recipients' performance of the training objectives: • Meets the prescribed <u>standards</u> • Is done under the prescribed <u>conditions</u> • Uses the designated <u>processes</u> • Achieves the desired <u>functions</u> • Incorporates all of the required <u>components</u>
4 CONDITIONS	At Level 4, recipients' performance of the training objectives: • Does not meet the prescribed standards • Is done under the prescribed <u>conditions</u> • Uses the designated <u>processes</u> • Achieves the desired <u>functions</u> • Incorporates all of the required <u>components</u>
3 PROCESSES	At Level 3, recipients' performance of the training objectives: • Does not meet the prescribed standards • Is not done under prescribed conditions • Uses the designated <u>processes</u> • Achieves the desired <u>functions</u> • Incorporates all of the required <u>components</u>
2 FUNCTIONS	At Level 2, recipients' performance of the training objectives: • Does not meet the prescribed standards • Is not done under prescribed conditions • Does not use the designated processes • Achieves the desired <u>functions</u> • Incorporates all of the required <u>components</u>
1 COMPONENTS	At Level 1, recipients' performance of the training objectives: • Does not meet the prescribed standards • Is not done under prescribed conditions • Does not use the designated processes • Does not achieve the desired functions • Incorporates all of the required <u>components</u>

Table 7.

DEVELOPING WELL-DEFINED APPLICATION INDICES

	LEVELS	QUESTIONS TO BE ANSWERED	EXAMPLE INDICES
5	STANDARDS	. How well should the objective be performed? . How will you know that the objective has been performed at the prescribed level of excellence?	. Word processing trainees will produce a 40-page document that: - Meets prescribed format and layout conventions (e.g., spacing, margins, type style) - Has no content missing - Has less than 8 typos . The documents will be judged by a trained proofreader.
4	CONDITIONS	. Where and when should the objective be performed? . How will you know that the objective was performed under the prescribed conditions?	. Word processing trainees will complete the assignment in one work day while in a typical office setting that includes the following distractions: - Answer and refer 10 phone calls per hour - Help another worker to reorder a dropped document - Handle a floppy disk salesperson . Observe to ensure that the prescribed conditions were present.
3	PROCESSES	. What processes or special methods should be used to perform the objective? . How will you know that the processes or special methods were used correctly?	. Word processing trainees will use all software functions of the word processing system (e.g., coding, storing, etc.) properly. . Expert word processing personnel will be able to edit and manipulate the trainees' disks.

69

Continued . . .

Table 7 (Continued)

DEVELOPING WELL-DEFINED APPLICATION INDICES

	LEVELS	QUESTIONS TO BE ANSWERED	EXAMPLE INDICES
2	FUNCTIONS	. What function should the performance of the objective fulfill? . How will you know if the function was met?	. Word processing trainees will produce a 40-page, double-spaced document. . Review the document generated.
1	COMPONENTS	. What essential ingredients should be used when performing the objective? . How will you know if the ingredients were present?	. Word processing trainees will use the XYZ system and software. . Observe the word processing trainees actually using the XYZ system and software.

Are There Other Ways To Assess Application?

Rating recipient performance in a simulation is the preferred approach for assessing skill application. If this approach is not feasible, then subjective data may be collected. For example, we may collect opinion data from the recipients on whether or not they think they can use their skills to achieve the training objectives. Table 8 presents a sample subjective rating scale for measuring recipients' attitudes concerning their ability to apply a newly acquired skill.

How Are Application Data Used During Training Delivery?

Skill application data generated during a training session can be used by training delivery personnel to make adjustments in the application exercises.

Exercising does not introduce any new training content. During the exercise, recipients are given an opportunity to practice the skills over and over until they acquire them. Recipients must also be given an opportunity to practice applying the skills during the exercise portion of the training. The application exercises simulate the conditions stated in the training objective.

If the training recipients have acquired the content but fail to apply their skills to the training objective, then the trainer may need to modify the application exercises. A trainer may modify the application exercises by:

- Gradually introducing conditions for performing the skill.

- Sequencing the application exercises from the least to most difficult.

- Gradually removing prompts or assistance as the recipients demonstrate increasingly more difficult applications.

Table 8.

SAMPLE SUBJECTIVE APPLICATION RATING SCALE

- RATINGS -

RATE HOW CONFIDENT YOU FEEL ABOUT USING YOUR WORD PROCESSING SKILLS:	Not Confident $\longrightarrow$ Very Confident				
COMPONENTS					
1. Using the XYZ system and software	1	2	3	4	5
FUNCTIONS					
2. To produce a 40-page, double-spaced document using the XYZ system and software.	1	2	3	4	5
PROCESSES					
3. To produce a 40-page, double-spaced document using all of the software functions accurately on the XYZ system.	1	2	3	4	5
CONDITIONS					
4. To produce a 40-page, double-spaced document using all of the software functions accurately on the XYZ system in a busy office setting over the course of an 8-hour day.	1	2	3	4	5
STANDARDS					
5. To do everything described in item 4 and meet the following standards: • The document layout and format will meet conventions. • No content will be missing. • There will be less than 8 typo's.	1	2	3	4	5

How Are Application Data Used During Instructional Design?

Skill application data can be used to modify existing instructional designs. If the recipients acquire the content but fail to apply it to the training objectives, then we must look for weaknesses in our content development and delivery plan.

DESIGN TASK	USE APPLICATION DATA TO . . .
DEVELOP CONTENT	• Determine if the skills, skill steps, and supportive knowledge lead to the achievement of the training objectives. • Modify weaknesses in existing training content.
PLAN DELIVERY	• Determine if sufficient application exercises are planned. • Determine if the sequence of the application exercises is appropriate. • Determine if the application exercises systematically lead the recipients through increasingly more difficult levels of skill applications. • Modify weaknesses in the application exercises.

Summary

However you choose to measure recipient skill application, the essential question to be answered is: Did the recipients apply the training content to the dimensions of the training objective?

Continued . . .

Summary
(Continued)

In planning your assessment of recipient skill application, remember to complete the following planning steps:

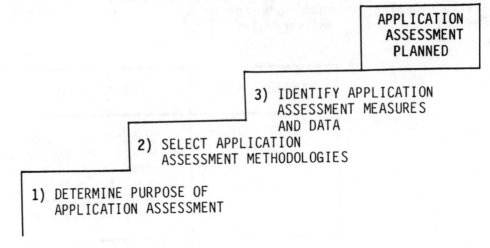

APPLICATION
ASSESSMENT
PLANNED

3) IDENTIFY APPLICATION
ASSESSMENT MEASURES
AND DATA

2) SELECT APPLICATION
ASSESSMENT METHODOLOGIES

1) DETERMINE PURPOSE OF
APPLICATION ASSESSMENT

- PLANNING JOB AID -

STEP 1: DETERMINE THE PURPOSE

- The purpose of the application
  assessment is: ☐ Summative   ☐ Formative

STEP 2: SELECT THE METHODOLOGIES

- The evaluation design will be: ☐ Experimental   ☐ Naturalistic

- Data collection will be: ☐ Static: Indicate When _____
                             ☐ Dynamic: Indicate When _____

STEP 3: IDENTIFY MEASURES AND DATA

- The types of measures to be used   ☐ Criterion-Referenced
  are: ☐ Norm-Referenced

- The types of data to be collect-
  ed are: ☐ Objective   ☐ Subjective

- Will a favorability scale be used? ☐ Yes   ☐ No

  IF YES . . . Construct your application assessment scale.

  LEVELS   INDICES

5

4

3

2

1

- PLANNING JOB AID -

APPLICATION SIMULATION OUTLINE
COMPONENTS: Describe who and what needs to be available during the simulation.
FUNCTIONS: Describe what will be done by the recipients during the simulation.
PROCESSES: Describe the specific procedures, special methods, and/or activities to be used by recipients.
CONDITIONS: Describe the environmental (setting, distractions, etc.) and time factors to be imposed on the recipients during the simulation.
STANDARDS: Describe the level of excellence to be achieved by recipients during the simulation.

ASSESSING TASK TRANSFER

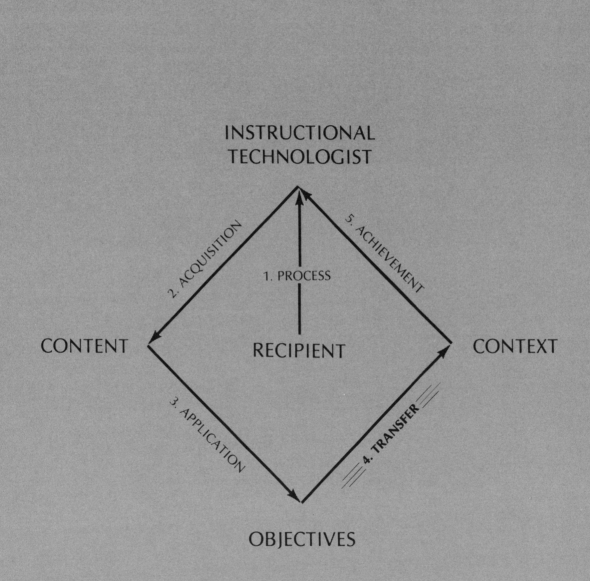

What Is Assessing Task Transfer?

The essential task in assessing task transfer is to determine if the recipients used their skills to accomplish the tasks required by the real-life context (i.e., work setting). The transfer assessment answers the question: Did the recipients transfer the training content to the dimensions of their real-life contextual tasks?

What Are The Dimensions Of Task Performance?

The dimensions of task performance are directly analogous to the dimensions used in specifying our training objectives.

DIMENSIONS OF TASK PERFORMANCE

COMPONENTS:	Who and what things will be involved in performing the tasks?
FUNCTIONS:	What activities will result from performing the tasks?
PROCESSES:	How will the tasks be performed?
CONDITIONS:	Where and when will the tasks be performed?
STANDARDS:	How well will the tasks be performed?

How Does Application Differ From Transfer?

The only difference between measuring recipient skill application and recipient task transfer is the conditions under which the assessment takes place.

ASSESSMENT	CONDITIONS
Application	• The assessment is based on recipient skill performance in a simulation. • The simulation is planned and controlled by the evaluator.
Transfer	• The assessment is based on recipient task performance in the real-life context. • The real-life context is usually not controlled or manipulated by the evaluator.

79

| How Is Task Transfer Measured? | Task transfer can be measured using a developmental scale to rate recipient performance in their real-life contexts (i.e., work settings). Remember, a developmental scale is a form of favorability scaling (see the Appendix of this volume for a description of scaling techniques). |

TASK TRANSFER SCALE

LEVELS

5	STANDARDS	Did the recipients' performance of their contextual tasks meet pre-scribed standards?
4	CONDITIONS	Did the recipients' performance of their contextual tasks occur under the prescribed conditions?
3	PROCESSES	Did the recipients' performance of their contextual tasks involve the prescribed methods?
2	FUNCTIONS	Did the recipients' performance of their contextual tasks achieve the desired activities or purposes?
1	COMPONENTS	Did the recipients' performance of their contextual tasks incorporate all of the basic ingredients?

Table 9 presents a further explanation of the task transfer scale.

| What Are The Task Transfer Indices? | Behavioral indices for task transfer should already exist. In a well-planned training design, the behavioral indices for task performance are built into the training objectives. The behavioral indices in the training objectives must directly correspond to the behavioral indices of task performance. An assessment of task transfer is less valuable when the performance expectations of the context are different from the performance expectations within the training objectives. Therefore, it is strongly recommended that the behavioral indices used to assess application are also used to assess transfer. See Table 7, Developing Well-Defined Application Indices, for examples of application indices. |

Table 9.

UNDERSTANDING THE TASK TRANSFER SCALE

LEVELS	EXPLANATION
5 STANDARDS	At Level 5, recipients' task performance: . Meets the prescribed standards . Is done under the prescribed conditions . Uses the designated processes . Achieves the desired functions . Incorporates all of the required components
4 CONDITIONS	At Level 4, recipients' task performance: . Does not meet the prescribed standards . Is done under the prescribed conditions . Uses the designated processes . Achieves the desired functions . Incorporates all of the required components
3 PROCESSES	At Level 3, recipients' task performance: . Does not meet the prescribed standards . Is not done under the prescribed conditions . Uses the designated processes . Achieves the desired functions . Incorporates all of the required components
2 FUNCTIONS	At Level 2, recipients' task performance: . Does not meet the prescribed standards . Is not done under the prescribed conditions . Does not use the designated processes . Achieves the desired functions . Incorporates all of the required components
1 COMPONENTS	At Level 1, recipients' task performance: . Does not meet the prescribed standards . Is not done under the prescribed conditions . Does not use the designated processes . Does not achieve the desired functions . Incorporates all of the required components

**Can A Transfer
Criterion Be
Established?**

A criterion is built into the task transfer scale. The criterion is LEVEL 5: STANDARDS. If the recipients fail to reach the standard of excellence required by their context, then it follows that the work unit will not be able to fully execute their key result areas. In turn, the work unit's failure to execute the key result areas will most likely affect the achievement of the original productivity goals.

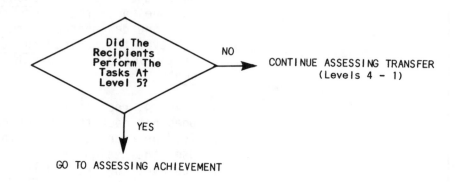

**Are There Other
Ways To Assess
Transfer?**

Rating recipients' performance in their real-life context using criterion-referenced measures is the preferred approach for assessing task transfers. If this approach is not feasible, then:

● You may want to use existing measures of task performance (e.g., performance appraisal reports, anecdotal records, work measurement logs, etc.).

● You may want to collect opinion data regarding task performance from recipients and their supervisors.

A sample subjective rating scale appears in Table 10.

Table 10.

SAMPLE SUBJECTIVE TRANSFER RATING SCALES

I. RECIPIENT RATINGS

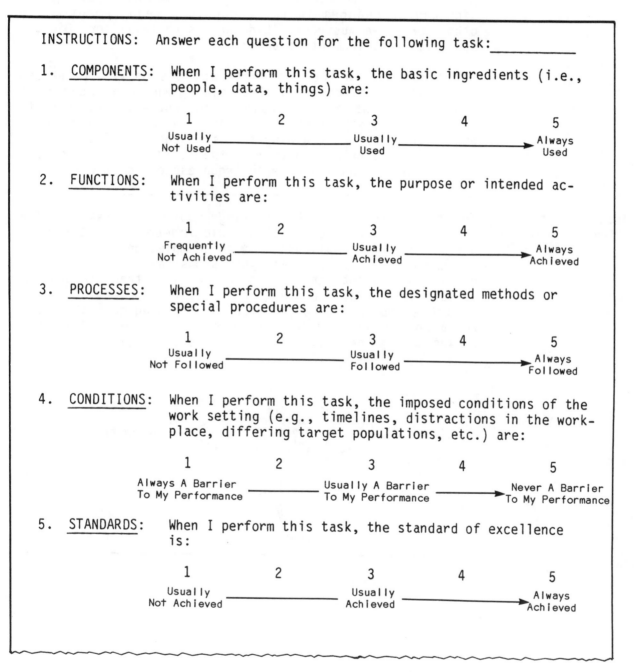

INSTRUCTIONS: Answer each question for the following task: _____

1. COMPONENTS: When I perform this task, the basic ingredients (i.e., people, data, things) are:

1	2	3	4	5
Usually Not Used		Usually Used		Always Used

2. FUNCTIONS: When I perform this task, the purpose or intended activities are:

1	2	3	4	5
Frequently Not Achieved		Usually Achieved		Always Achieved

3. PROCESSES: When I perform this task, the designated methods or special procedures are:

1	2	3	4	5
Usually Not Followed		Usually Followed		Always Followed

4. CONDITIONS: When I perform this task, the imposed conditions of the work setting (e.g., timelines, distractions in the workplace, differing target populations, etc.) are:

1	2	3	4	5
Always A Barrier To My Performance		Usually A Barrier To My Performance		Never A Barrier To My Performance

5. STANDARDS: When I perform this task, the standard of excellence is:

1	2	3	4	5
Usually Not Achieved		Usually Achieved		Always Achieved

How Are Transfer Data Used?

Task transfer data are used to modify existing instructional designs. If the recipients applied the content but fail to transfer it to the performance of contextual tasks, then we must look for weaknesses in our original instructional design and/or changes in the contextual requirements. In other words, we must ask: Did our design fail? or, Did the contextual requirements change?

Modifications in the instructional design will be needed under either circumstance. Determining why the recipients failed to transfer the training content will assist us to select the proper corrective action. Figure 2 illustrates how to troubleshoot training transfer problems. The troubleshooting guide helps you to make the least costly fix possible. An explanation of each troubleshooting step follows.

Troubleshooting
Step 1: Verify Application

The first step in troubleshooting problems in task transfer is to verify that the recipients did indeed reach the criterion for skill application by the completion of the training experience. If your analysis shows that the application criterion was not achieved, then the first transfer problem to address is that recipients are leaving the training experience unprepared to transfer the training content. When recipients fail to apply their skills, we must look for weaknesses in the training content and the delivery plan.

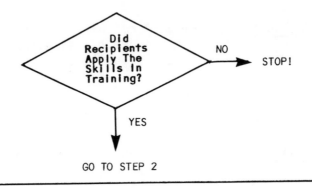

Figure 2.

TROUBLESHOOTING TRAINING TRANSFER PROBLEMS

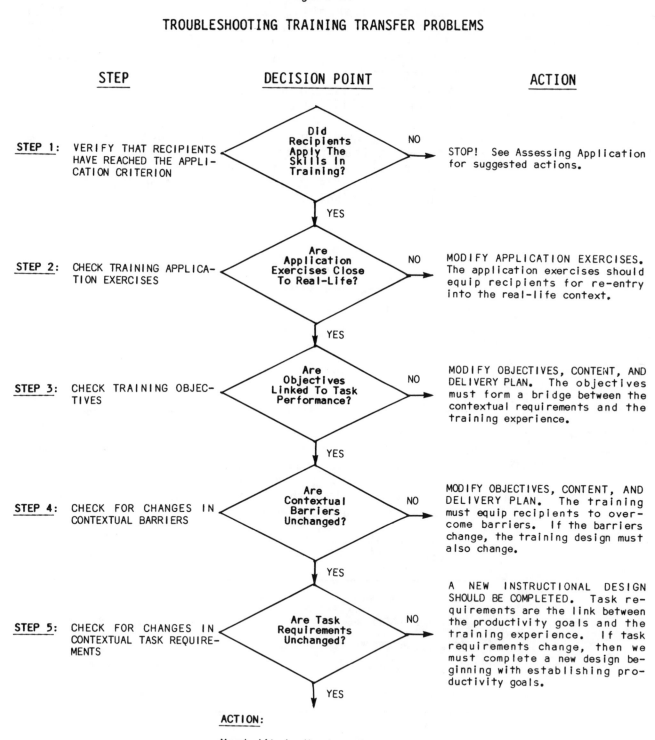

	STEP	DECISION POINT	ACTION
STEP 1:	VERIFY THAT RECIPIENTS HAVE REACHED THE APPLICATION CRITERION	Did Recipients Apply The Skills In Training? — NO →	STOP! See Assessing Application for suggested actions.
STEP 2:	CHECK TRAINING APPLICATION EXERCISES	Are Application Exercises Close To Real-Life? — NO →	MODIFY APPLICATION EXERCISES. The application exercises should equip recipients for re-entry into the real-life context.
STEP 3:	CHECK TRAINING OBJECTIVES	Are Objectives Linked To Task Performance? — NO →	MODIFY OBJECTIVES, CONTENT, AND DELIVERY PLAN. The objectives must form a bridge between the contextual requirements and the training experience.
STEP 4:	CHECK FOR CHANGES IN CONTEXTUAL BARRIERS	Are Contextual Barriers Unchanged? — NO →	MODIFY OBJECTIVES, CONTENT, AND DELIVERY PLAN. The training must equip recipients to overcome barriers. If the barriers change, the training design must also change.
STEP 5:	CHECK FOR CHANGES IN CONTEXTUAL TASK REQUIREMENTS	Are Task Requirements Unchanged? — NO →	A NEW INSTRUCTIONAL DESIGN SHOULD BE COMPLETED. Task requirements are the link between the productivity goals and the training experience. If task requirements change, then we must complete a new design beginning with establishing productivity goals.

ACTION:

Most likely the transfer problem is not an instructional problem. Recommend that a consulting intervention be conducted.

85

Troubleshooting
Step 2: Check
Application
Exercises

Our next troubleshooting step is to check the application exercises used in training. A common problem encountered by training recipients is that the real-life context is dissimilar to the simulated context or practice environment used during the training exercises. The recipients are able to apply their skills during the simulation but unable to perform in the real-life context.

If our training simulations don't approximate the real-life setting, then transfer problems may result. The second troubleshooting step is to make sure that training delivery plans provide recipients with a series of application exercises that increasingly approximate the real-life context.

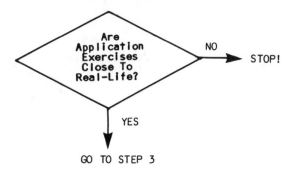

Troubleshooting
Step 3: Check
Objectives

The third troubleshooting step is to check the training objectives. The training objectives link the contextual requirements to the training experience. If the training objectives are not consistent with the contextual requirements, then it follows that mastery of the training content will not lead to task transfer.

DO . . . TRAINING OBJECTIVES	=	TASK REQUIREMENTS ?
DO . . . STANDARDS	=	STANDARDS ?
DO . . . CONDITIONS	=	CONDITIONS ?
DO . . . PROCESSES	=	PROCESSES ?
DO . . . FUNCTIONS	=	FUNCTIONS ?
DO . . . COMPONENTS	=	COMPONENTS ?

Continued . . .

**Troubleshooting
Step 3
(Continued)**

By checking our training objectives, we ensure that task transfer is possible. Accurate, well-defined training objectives are a necessary but not sufficient condition for task transfer.

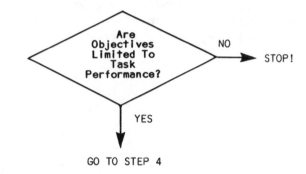

GO TO STEP 4

**Troubleshooting
Step 4: Check
Barriers**

Next, we review the barriers to task performance. The barriers should have been assessed during the instructional design phase. Remember, contextual barriers are any sources which prevent the performance of the tasks.

BARRIER DIMENSIONS

BARRIER SOURCES	PHYSICAL	EMOTIONAL	INTELLECTUAL
PERSONNEL	Capacity?	Motives?	Skills?
ENVIRONMENT	Resources?	Incentives?	Procedures?
INFORMATION	Tasks?	Mission?	Flow?

Continued . . .

**Troubleshooting
Step 4
(Continued)**

The training objectives and the training content should be designed to equip recipients to overcome the contextual barriers. The recipients should practice overcoming these barriers during the training application exercises. If the contextual barriers change, then the training experience may need to be modified. An unexpected change in contextual barriers can influence recipient task transfer.

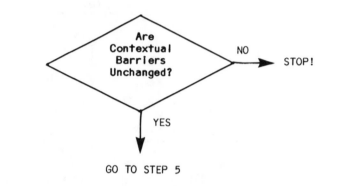

**Troubleshooting
Step 5: Check Tasks**

The final troubleshooting step is to make sure that the task requirements have not changed since we designed the instructional intervention. Remember, the tasks are identified by analyzing the planning, producing, and assessing processes performed by the recipients within each of their key result areas.

PLANNING ⟶ PRODUCING ⟶ ASSESSING

If the current task requirements are discrepant from the tasks identified during the instructional design, then it follows that recipient task transfer is unlikely. When changes have occurred in contextual requirements, we must redesign the instructional intervention. We must recycle the entire design process including a review of the current productivity goals. Changes in contextual requirements can greatly affect productivity goal achievement.

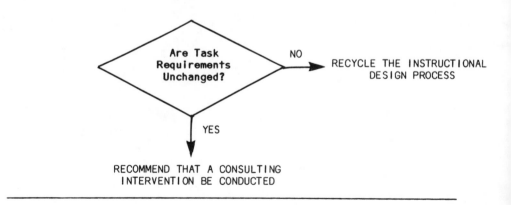

What Is A Consulting Intervention?

Volume I of this series presents an overview of a consulting intervention. The consulting intervention is illustrated below.

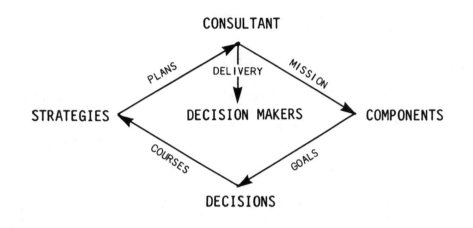

Summary

However you choose to measure recipient task transfer, the essential question to be answered is: Did the recipients transfer the training content to the dimensions of their real-life contextual tasks?

In planning our assessment of recipient task transfer, remember to complete the following planning steps.

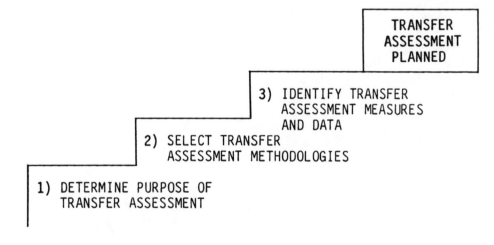

- PLANNING JOB AID -

STEP 1: DETERMINE THE PURPOSE

- The purpose of the transfer
  assessment is: ☐ Summative   ☐ Formative

STEP 2: SELECT THE METHODOLOGIES

- The evaluation design will be: ☐ Experimental   ☐ Naturalistic

- Data collection will be: ☐ Static: Indicate When _____
      ☐ Dynamic: Indicate When _____

STEP 3: IDENTIFY MEASURES AND DATA

- The types of measures to be used   ☐ Criterion-Referenced
  are: ☐ Norm-Referenced

- The types of data to be collected are: ☐ Objective   ☐ Subjective

- Will a favorability scale be used? ☐ Yes   ☐ No

  IF YES . . . Construct your transfer assessment scale.

  <u>LEVELS</u>   <u>INDICES</u>

5

4

3

2

1

ASSESSING CONTEXTUAL BARRIERS
- JOB AID -

	PHYSICAL	EMOTIONAL	INTELLECTUAL
P E R S O N N E L	CAPACITY ☐ Lack of Strength ☐ Lack of Dexterity ☐ Lack of Stamina ☐ Lack of Attentiveness ☐ Lack of Concentration ☐ Inability to Learn New Tasks	MOTIVES ☐ Lack of Internalized Reward System ☐ Lack of Personalized Goals ☐ Lack of Initiative ☐ Personnel Values Inconsistent With Mission	SKILLS/KNOWLEDGE ☐ Lack of Basic Skills ☐ Lack of Specific Task-Related Skills ☐ Inadequate Knowledge of Procedures and Policies ☐ Inadequate Understanding of Supportive Knowledge
E N V I R O N M E N T	RESOURCES ☐ Inadequate Personnel ☐ Inadequate Raw Materials ☐ Inadequate Supplies ☐ Inadequate Equipment ☐ Inadequate Space ☐ Inadequate Support Services ☐ Inadequate Energy	INCENTIVES ☐ Good Performance Is Not Positively Reinforced ☐ Poor Performance Is Positively Reinforced ☐ Poor Performance Is Not Linked to Negative Consequences	PROCEDURES/METHODS ☐ Out-of-Date Materials ☐ Unreasonable Deadline ☐ Unclear Chain of Command ☐ Unclear Reporting Structure ☐ Lack of Access to Decision Process ☐ Work Not Oriented to Performers ☐ Extensive Paperwork/ Red Tape
I N F O R M A T I O N	TASK EXPECTATIONS ☐ Inconsistent Task Requirements ☐ Conflicting Time Demands ☐ Inadequate Task Assignment ☐ Unnecessarily Complex Tasks ☐ Duplicative Task Assignments ☐ Infrequently Used Tasks	MISSION ☐ No Policy ☐ Conflicting Policies ☐ Changing Policies ☐ Conflicting Assignment ☐ Organizational Goals Inconsistent With Mission	INFORMATION FLOW ☐ Changing Information ☐ Lack of Information ☐ Lack of Accurate Data ☐ Lack of Timely Data ☐ Lack of Complete Data ☐ Lack of Feedback ☐ Lack of Monitoring

NOTE: Compare the results of this barrier assessment with the barrier assessment completed during the instructional design phase.

ASSESSING GOAL ACHIEVEMENT

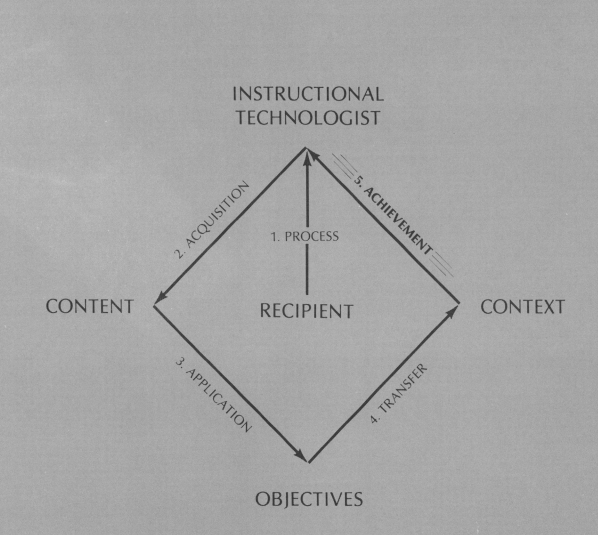

What Is Assessing Goal Achievement?

The essential task in assessing goal achievement is to determine if the recipients achieved the productivity goals. We began our intervention by establishing productivity goals and now have come full circle. Our final task is to assess our productivity outcomes. Remember, the reason for the original instructional design is to achieve productivity outcomes. The goal achievement assessment answers the question: Did the recipients achieve the productivity goals?

What Are Productivity Goals?

Productivity goals individualize the overall organizational mission to the units targeted for the instructional intervention. The productivity goals are stated in terms of results outputs and/or resource inputs.

$$\text{PRODUCTIVITY GOALS} = \frac{\text{RESULTS OUTPUTS (RO)}}{\text{RESOURCE INPUTS (RI)}}$$

Our first instructional design task was to establish desired goal levels for both the results outputs and resource inputs.

What Are Goal Levels?

A goal level is simply the amount of desired change to occur in the results outputs (RO) and/or resource inputs (RI). The way in which we set our goal levels influences the anticipated outcomes.

Typically, our goals may be grouped into the following categories:

- INCREMENTAL
- EFFECTIVENESS

- EFFICIENCY
- MAINTENANCE

What Are Incremental Goals?

Ideally, goal levels should be established to achieve incremental productivity gains. Incremental goal levels are expressed as follows:

RO+
RI-

SET TARGETS FOR INCREASED RESULTS OUTPUTS, and
SET TARGETS FOR DECREASED RESOURCE INPUTS

Incremental goals are achieved when the recipients' work unit increases results outputs (RO+) while decreasing resource inputs (RI-).

**What Are
Effectiveness
Goals?**

Often, ideal goal levels are not possible. Frequently, our goals focus on increasing the work unit's effectiveness. Effectiveness goal levels are expressed as follows:

SET TARGETS FOR INCREASED RESULTS OUTPUTS, and
SET TARGETS FOR MAINTAINED RESOURCE INPUTS

Effectiveness goals are achieved when the recipients' work unit increases results outputs (RO+) while maintaining resource inputs (RI°).

**What Are
Efficiency
Goals?**

In some cases, work units are reaching desired levels of results outputs but need to decrease resource inputs. Under these circumstances, efficiency goals are established. Efficiency goal levels are expressed as follows:

SET TARGETS FOR MAINTAINED RESULTS OUTPUTS, and
SET TARGETS FOR DECREASED RESOURCE INPUTS

Efficiency goals are achieved when the recipients' work unit maintains results outputs while decreasing resource inputs.

**What Are
Maintenance
Goals?**

Infrequently, goals are established for maintaining the current relationships between results outputs and resource inputs. Maintenance goal levels are expressed as follows:

SET TARGETS FOR MAINTAINED RESULTS OUTPUTS, and
SET TARGETS FOR MAINTAINED RESOURCE INPUTS

Maintenance goals are achieved when the recipients' work unit maintains a balanced relationship between current levels of results outputs (RO°) and resource inputs (RI°).

Can Other Types Of Goals Be Set?

In very rare instances, goal levels may be set so that the resource inputs exceed the results outputs. This inverse of resources and results may be appropriate to resolve short-term performance crises. For example, sales continue to decline while a new product line is under development. A short-term intervention is needed to prevent further decline of the old product line while the development work is completed on the new product line.

This type of goal is called inefficiency and is expressed as follows:

$$\frac{RO°}{RI+}$$ SET TARGETS FOR MAINTAINED RESULTS OUTPUTS, and
SET TARGETS FOR INCREASED RESOURCE INPUTS

The achievement of an inefficiency goal is really a marginal achievement. Ultimately, only productive organizations will thrive and grow. The achievement of an inefficiency goal should be considered only a short-term survival gain.

How Is Goal Achievement Assessed?

Goal achievement is assessed by comparing current productivity levels with desired productivity levels. When the current productivity level meets or exceeds the desired productivity level, then we have achieved our goals.

GOAL ACHIEVEMENT =

CURRENT PRODUCTIVITY LEVEL	>	DESIRED PRODUCTIVITY LEVEL

How Are
Productivity
Levels
Assessed?

In order to assess goal achievement, we must first assess the productivity of the recipients' work units. Productivity can be assessed using a favorability scale. (See the Appendix of this volume for a description of scaling techniques.)

PRODUCTIVITY SCALE

LEVELS

5	INCREMENTAL	Were results outputs increased while resource inputs decreased?
4	EFFECTIVENESS	Were results outputs increased while maintaining resource inputs?
	OR	
	EFFICIENCY	Were results outputs maintained while decreasing resource inputs?
3	MAINTENANCE	Were results outputs and resource inputs maintained?
2	INEFFECTIVENESS	Were results outputs decreased while maintaining resource inputs?
	OR	
	INEFFICIENCY	Were results outputs maintained while increasing resource inputs?
1	DECREMENTAL	Were results outputs decreased while increasing resource inputs?

A further explanation of the productivity scale appears in Table 11.

Table 11.

UNDERSTANDING THE PRODUCTIVITY SCALE

	LEVELS	EXPLANATION	
5	INCREMENTAL	At Level 5, recipients' work units:	
		• Increased results outputs, and • Decreased resource inputs	$\dfrac{RO+}{RI-}$
4	EFFECTIVENESS	At Level 4, recipients' work units:	
		• Increased results outputs, and • Maintained resource inputs	$\dfrac{RO+}{RI°}$
		OR	
	EFFICIENCY	• Maintained results outputs, and • Decreased resource inputs	$\dfrac{RO°}{RI-}$
3	MAINTENANCE	At Level 3, recipients' work units:	
		• Maintained results outputs, and • Maintained resource inputs	$\dfrac{RO°}{RI°}$
2	INEFFECTIVENESS	At Level 2, recipients' work units:	
		• Decreased results outputs, and • Maintained resource inputs	$\dfrac{RO-}{RI°}$
		OR	
	INEFFICIENCY	• Maintained results outputs, and • Increased resource inputs	$\dfrac{RO°}{RI+}$
1	DECREMENTAL	At Level 1, recipients' work units:	
		• Decreased results outputs, and • Increased resource inputs	$\dfrac{RO-}{RI+}$

NOTE: The productivity scale is unlike the scales used in the previous assessment levels. The other scales presented were developmental or cumulative. To reach a level on a developmental scale, the performer must have achieved all subsequent performance levels. The levels on the productivity scale are independent of one another.

**What Are The
Productivity
Indices?**

In a comprehensive instructional design, productivity indices were identified when establishing the productivity
goals. The indices identified were for both the results
outputs and resource inputs. It is strongly recommended
that the productivity indices used to assess preintervention
levels of productivity be used to assess postintervention
levels of productivity. A review of results outputs indices
and resource inputs indices follows.

**What Are Results
Outputs Indices?**

Results outputs can be assessed using quantitative and/or
qualitative indices. Following are the quantitative and
qualitative indices that can be used to assess preintervention and postintervention results outputs:

QUANTITATIVE INDICES	QUALITATIVE INDICES
Volume: How many? **Rate**: How many per time unit? **Timeliness**: On time?	**Accuracy**: How well? Meet standards? **Functionality**: Does it work? **Initiative**: Is it new?

Combined quantitative/qualitative measures may be used to
assess results outputs. Ideally, results output indices
should be translated into dollar values.

**What Are Resource
Inputs Indices?**

Developing indices for resource inputs simply involves identifying the critical financial and nonfinancial expenditures
made for:

PERSONNEL ● INFORMATION ● CAPITAL

An actual or approximate dollar value is then attached to
each resource input.

Can Simple Indices Be Used?

Often, the instructional designer has neither the resources nor the ability to access data about every resource input. Sometimes measuring all dimensions of results outputs can be extremely complex. When confronted with these barriers, the instructional designer should simplify the productivity indices. For example, if the major resource expended is staff time, then it might be wise to use this as the main index of productivity. Table 12 presents a simplified approach for converting results obtained to hours saved.

The key is to establish the critical few productivity indices that account for the greatest impact on goal achievement.

Can An Achievement Criterion Be Established?

The criterion for goal achievement must be established by the instructional designer based upon the original goal levels established at the onset of the intervention. The following table is designed to help in the selection of your achievement criterion.

IF ORIGINAL GOAL WAS. . .		THEN THE CRITERION IS. . .
INCREMENTAL	$\dfrac{RO+}{RI-}$	Level 5
EFFECTIVENESS	$\dfrac{RO+}{RI^\circ}$	Level 4
EFFICIENCY	$\dfrac{RO^\circ}{RI-}$	Level 4
MAINTENANCE	$\dfrac{RO^\circ}{RI^\circ}$	Level 3

Table 12.

SIMPLIFIED APPROACH USING TIME SAVED AS A PRODUCTIVITY INDEX

STEPS	EXAMPLES
STEP 1: IDENTIFY RESULTS For each result obtained, answer the question: "Because this result was achieved, what was the time saved?"	New procedures enabled personnel to increase output from an average of 12 to 20 documents per day.

STEP 2: DETERMINE AVERAGE TIME SAVED
                PER INSTANCE
    For each instance or event, determine the average time saved by all personnel including delivery personnel, supervisors, etc.
	Average time saved per document completed was 1 hour.

STEP 3: DETERMINE NUMBER OF INSTANCES Now, determine how often the instances occur.	800 documents were produced.
STEP 4: DETERMINE EXTRA TIME REQUIRED Next, determine if extra time was required to obtain the results.	80 hours were used to plan the new procedures.
STEP 5: CALCULATE THE TOTAL TIME SAVED Calculate the total time savings as follows: AVERAGE × NUMBER − EXTRA = TOTAL TIME OF TIME/ TIME SAVED INSTANCES RESOURCES SAVED	1 HOUR 800 AVG. TIME × NUMBER OF − SAVED INSTANCES 80 HOURS 720 HOURS ADDITIONAL = TOTAL TIME HOURS SAVED

STEP 6: CONVERT THE TIME SAVINGS TO DOLLAR
                SAVINGS
    Financially convert the time savings to a dollar value as follows:
 	
AVERAGE   TOTAL TIME   TOTAL
HOURLY COSTS ×   SAVED   =   SAVINGS
	\$20.00 720 HOURS \$14,400
	AVERAGE × TOTAL TIME = TOTAL
	HOURLY COST SAVED SAVINGS

How Are Scale Levels Used?

All levels of productivity scales can be used in relation to the selected criterion. For example, if the criterion is Level 4: Effectiveness/Efficiency, then we use the scale as follows:

When **Level 4** is the criterion, then . . .

Level 5 } Tells us we exceeded our goals.

Level 4 } Tells us goals were achieved.

Level 3
Level 2 } Tells us goals were not achieved. Each individual level tells us how far we are from achieving the goals.
Level 1

Are There Other Ways To Assess Achievement?

Assessing goal achievement using objective data is the preferred approach. If this approach is not feasible, then attitudinal data about goal achievement can be collected from decision makers. Table 13 presents sample subjective rating items for assessing productivity goal achievement.

Table 13.

SAMPLE SUBJECTIVE ACHIEVEMENT SCALE

INSTRUCTIONS: Select a rating that most closely describes the performance of the following work unit: _____

RESULTS OUTPUTS

. Quality standards for results are:

1	2	3	4	5
Usually Not Achieved		Usually Achieved		Usually Exceeded

. Quantity standards for results are:

1	2	3	4	5
Usually Not Achieved		Usually Achieved		Usually Exceeded

. Timelines for results are:

1	2	3	4	5
Usually Not Achieved		Usually Achieved		Usually Exceeded

RESOURCE INPUTS

. Personnel resource expenditures:

1	2	3	4	5
Usually Exceed Budget		Usually Are Within Budget		Usually Are Less Than Budget

. Information resource expenditures:

1	2	3	4	5
Usually Exceed Budget		Usually Are Within Budget		Usually Are Less Than Budget

. Capital resource expenditures:

1	2	3	4	5
Usually Exceed Budget		Usually Are Within Budget		Usually Are Less Than Budget

PRODUCTIVITY

. Since ____ / ____ / ____ , I feel that . . .

  . Results outputs have: ☐ Increased   ☐ Maintained   ☐ Decreased

  . Resource inputs have: ☐ Increased   ☐ Maintained   ☐ Decreased

**How Are
Achievement
Data Used?**

Achievement data can be used to ensure that our instructional designs contribute to the organization's productivity mission. Improving task performance on contextual requirements is a great achievement. However, if we improve task performance in the absence of goal achievement, then we have not fulfilled the larger organizational quest for productivity. Determining why the recipients failed to achieve their productivity goals will assist us to select the proper corrective action. Figure 3 illustrates how to troubleshoot goal achievement problems.

Troubleshooting
**Step 1: Verify
Transfer**

The first step in troubleshooting problems in goal achievement is to verify that the recipients did indeed reach the criterion for task transfer. If your analysis shows that the transfer criterion was not achieved, then your problem lies with recipient transfer. To achieve the productivity goals, we must first meet the contextual task requirements.

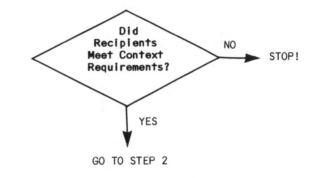

Figure 3.

TROUBLESHOOTING GOAL ACHIEVEMENT PROBLEMS

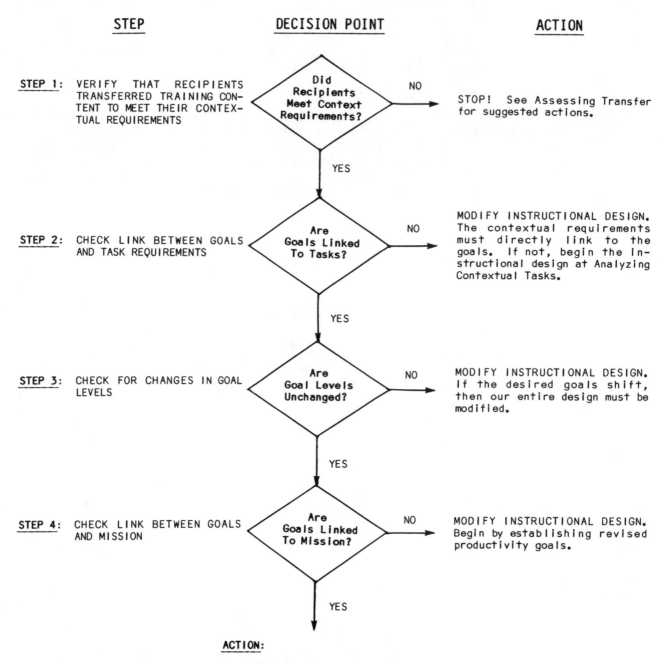

STEP	DECISION POINT	ACTION
STEP 1: VERIFY THAT RECIPIENTS TRANSFERRED TRAINING CONTENT TO MEET THEIR CONTEXTUAL REQUIREMENTS	Did Recipients Meet Context Requirements? — NO	STOP! See Assessing Transfer for suggested actions.
STEP 2: CHECK LINK BETWEEN GOALS AND TASK REQUIREMENTS	Are Goals Linked To Tasks? — NO	MODIFY INSTRUCTIONAL DESIGN. The contextual requirements must directly link to the goals. If not, begin the instructional design at Analyzing Contextual Tasks.
STEP 3: CHECK FOR CHANGES IN GOAL LEVELS	Are Goal Levels Unchanged? — NO	MODIFY INSTRUCTIONAL DESIGN. If the desired goals shift, then our entire design must be modified.
STEP 4: CHECK LINK BETWEEN GOALS AND MISSION	Are Goals Linked To Mission? — NO	MODIFY INSTRUCTIONAL DESIGN. Begin by establishing revised productivity goals.

ACTION:

Most likely, the goal achievement problem is out of your hands. Recommend that a consulting intervention be conducted.

106

Troubleshooting

Step 2: **Check Goal/**
Task Link

Our next troubleshooting step is to check the link established between the productivity goals and the contextual tasks. The achievement of our contextual tasks must lead to achievement of our productivity goals. Remember, our productivity goals set targets for resource inputs and results outputs. Tasks are the means by which the resource inputs are converted to results outputs.

RESOURCE INPUTS ⟶ PROCESSES ⟶ RESULTS OUTPUTS

Tasks

Productivity goals can only be achieved through the performance of the tasks required to convert resource inputs to results outputs. If we fail to identify all of the necessary tasks, then we must recycle our instructional design by beginning with an identification of the delivery, supervisory, and management tasks required to achieve our productivity goals.

Are Goals
Linked To
Tasks?

NO

STOP!

YES

GO TO STEP 3

Troubleshooting
  Step 3:   Check Goal
            Levels

The third troubleshooting step is to check the goal levels. In the Information Age, our data bases are in a constant state of flux due to the explosion of available information. Goal levels may have shifted while we were designing, implementing, and evaluating the instructional intervention.

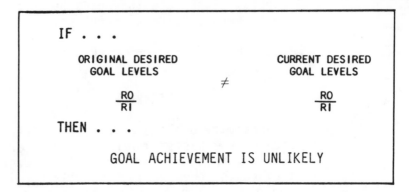

IF . . .

ORIGINAL DESIRED GOAL LEVELS		CURRENT DESIRED GOAL LEVELS
$\dfrac{RO}{RI}$	$\neq$	$\dfrac{RO}{RI}$

THEN . . .

GOAL ACHIEVEMENT IS UNLIKELY

When the goal levels have shifted, then we must recycle our entire instructional design.

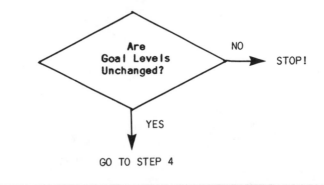

Are Goal Levels Unchanged?

NO → STOP!

YES

GO TO STEP 4

Editorial Note:
  Get Ready--
  Shifting Goals Are
  Becoming Status
  Quo

Shifting productivity goals will become increasingly common in the Information Age. The Information Age and the presence of shifting goal levels have the following profound implications for instructional designers:

- Traditional instructional evaluation will be replaced by constant feedback systems that emphasize dynamic data collection and interpretation.

Continued . . .

**Editorial Note
(Continued)**

- Traditional locked-step approaches to instructional design will be replaced by a dynamic systems approach that allows designers to efficiently recycle appropriate steps based upon a constant flow of new data.

- Instructional design and development processes will need to become increasingly efficient in order to avoid immediate obsolescence. Designers and developers will be able to avoid obsolescence only through improved utilization of human and information resources. Existing information technologies will need to be expanded and augmented by the emergence of human technologies.

Now for the good news . . . Instructional design in the Information Age will become an even more exciting and creative process. The demands of the Information Age will simultaneously challenge and free the skilled instructional technologist.

Troubleshooting
  **Step 4: Check Goal/
       Mission Link**

Our final troubleshooting step is to make sure that the productivity goals reflect the productivity mission or values of the overall organization. The productivity mission is identified and refined during the consulting intervention. Remember, an effective instructional intervention will be preceded by a consulting intervention. An instructional intervention will occur in a vacuum unless a current, well-articulated productivity mission exists. Assuming that a productivity mission does exist, then the productivity goals must directly contribute to the mission.

PRODUCTIVITY ⟶ PRODUCTIVITY
   GOALS   MISSION

Continued . . .

**Troubleshooting
Step 4
(Continued)**

If our original productivity goals for the instructional intervention do not contribute to the productivity mission, then ultimately we have failed. This is true even if "on paper" we have reached our original goals. In the eyes of the policy makers we have <u>not</u> achieved our goals and need to begin back at square one.

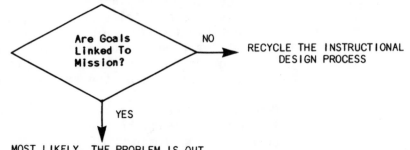

<u>NOTE</u>: See Volume I of this series for an overview of the consulting intervention process.

Summary

However you choose to measure productivity goal achievement, the essential question to be answered is: Did the recipients achieve the productivity goals?

In planning your assessment of productivity goal achievement, remember to complete the following planning steps:

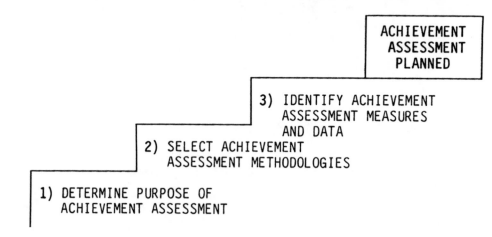

- PLANNING JOB AID -

STEP 1: DETERMINE THE PURPOSE

- The purpose of the achievement
  assessment is: ☐ Summative ☐ Formative

STEP 2: SELECT THE METHODOLOGIES

- The evaluation design will be: ☐ Experimental ☐ Naturalistic

- Data collection will be: ☐ Static: Indicate When_____
  ☐ Dynamic: Indicate When_____

STEP 3: IDENTIFY MEASURES AND DATA

- The types of measures to be used
  are: ☐ Criterion-Referenced
  ☐ Norm-Referenced

- The types of data to be collected are: ☐ Objective ☐ Subjective

- Will a favorability scale be used? ☐ Yes ☐ No

  IF YES . . . Construct your assessment scale.

LEVELS	INDICES	✓ YOUR CRITERION LEVEL
5	RO : —— RI :	☐
4	RO : —— RI :	☐
3	RO : —— RI :	☐
2	RO : —— RI :	☐
1	RO : —— RI :	☐

DEVELOPING INDICES FOR MEASURING RESULTS OUTPUTS

- PLANNING JOB AID -

STEP 1: SELECT TYPE OF INDICES

QUANTITATIVE   QUALITATIVE

☐ VOLUME   ☐ ACCURACY
☐ RATE   ☐ FUNCTIONALITY
☐ TIMELINESS   ☐ INITIATIVE

STEP 2: DESCRIBE HOW YOU WILL KNOW THAT RESULTS OUTPUTS WERE ACHIEVED

PROCESSING ASSESSMENT DATA

Summation

We made our instructional intervention in order to achieve our productivity goals. To do so, we: 1) established our productivity goals; 2) analyzed our contextual tasks; 3) specified our training objectives; 4) developed our training content; and 5) planned our training delivery.

After the training delivery, in reverse order, we assessed each instructional design stage: 1) recipient process movement; 2) recipient content acquisition; 3) recipient skill application; 4) recipient task transfer; and 5) productivity goal achievement. At each level, the basic questions in relation to the instructional intervention are the following: Did the recipients process, acquire, apply, and transfer the training content? At the goal achievement level, the question is: Did it make a difference?

In summation, we will discuss how the instructional designer/evaluator processes evaluation data to reach increasingly greater levels of productivity. The Age of Productivity demands outcome for every training dollar invested. Instructional evaluation must be in the service of productivity.

What Is Processing Evaluation Data?

An instructional evaluation is <u>not</u> complete until the instructional designer/evaluator <u>has</u> processed the resulting assessment data. Processing the assessment data directly parallels the training recipients' processes discussed in the section entitled, "Assessing Process Movement." To process assessment data, we <u>explore</u> our results, <u>understand</u> our goals, and <u>act</u> to achieve our goals.

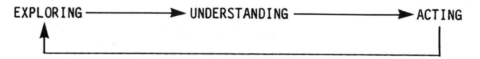

EXPLORING ⟶ UNDERSTANDING ⟶ ACTING

The remainder of this section presents suggestions for processing assessment data. Our own individual productivity depends on how well we process the assessment data resulting from our instructional interventions.

```
┌─────────────────────────────────────────┐
│                                         │
│              EXPLORING                  │
│                                         │
└─────────────────────────────────────────┘
```

What Is Exploring Assessment Data?

Our first step in processing the assessment data is to fully explore the data. Fully exploring the data means developing an overall picture of the data. In doing so, we bring together the individual assessments of each instructional design stage in order to form a single overall assessment. Our exploration of the data should tell us **"Where We Are."**

How Is An Overall Assessment Made?

An overall assessment of an instructional intervention can be made using a developmental scale. The overall intervention assessment scale is similar to the scales used to measure the individual assessment levels (i.e., process, acquisition, application, transfer, and achievement). In fact, the intervention assessment scale is built using the criterion level of all previous scales. The cumulative relationship among the individual assessment levels is reflected in the intervention assessment scale.

INTERVENTION ASSESSMENT SCALE

LEVELS

5	ACHIEVEMENT	Did we meet our productivity goal achievement criterion?
4	TRANSFER	Did we meet our task transfer criterion?
3	APPLICATION	Did we meet our skill application criterion?
2	ACQUISITION	Did we meet our content acquisition criterion?
1	PROCESS	Did we meet our recipient process movement criterion?

EXPLORING────────►UNDERSTANDING

**What Is
Understanding
Assessment
Data?**

Once we have explored the data and determined "Where We Are," we must next understand **"Where We Want Or Need To Be."** Understanding helps us to establish goals for:

- Further instructional interventions
                    - AND -
- Our own skill development.

The productivity of our organizations depends upon each intervention and intervener striving to achieve increasingly more productive goals. Our intervention results ultimately reflect our own productivity and skill levels. Understanding assessment data helps us to set personalized goals for our own skill improvement or refinement:

**How Are
Intervention
Goals Set?**

To set goals for further instructional interventions, we simply review the current level achieved and then determine where we want or need to be at the completion of our next intervention.

LEVEL ACHIEVED ON THIS INTERVENTION. . .	LEVEL TO BE ACHIEVED ON NEXT INTERVENTION. . .
<u>LEVELS</u>	<u>LEVELS</u>
☐ 5 ACHIEVEMENT	☐ 5 ACHIEVEMENT
☐ 4 TRANSFER	☐ 4 TRANSFER
☐ 3 APPLICATION	☐ 3 APPLICATION
☐ 2 ACQUISITION	☐ 2 ACQUISITION
☐ 1 PROCESS	☐ 1 PROCESS

**How Are Skill
Development
Goals Set?**

The results of our assessment can be used to target potential deficits in our instructional intervention skills.
Table 14 on the following pages will help you to understand
the relationship between the assessment data and potential
instructional intervention skill deficits. Setting a personal skill development goal involves clearly articulating
your deficit: "I am unable to_____." Next, you turn
your deficits into a goal statement: "I am unable
to_____, and I really want to improve my skills in this
area." When possible, state your skill goals in measurable
terms.

**Additional
Resources**

The authors of this volume have written the following additional publications. These publications may help you to
understand and set personal goals for improving your instructional intervention skills:

- ISD - Designing and Developing Instructional Systems.
  Volume I.

- TDS - Designing the Training Delivery. Volume I.

- TDS - Making the Training Delivery. Volume II.

Table 14.

UNDERSTANDING ASSESSMENT DATA: SETTING PERSONAL SKILL GOALS

ASSESSMENT LEVEL ACHIEVED	IMPLICATIONS	POTENTIAL DEFICITS IN INSTRUCTIONAL INTERVENTION SKILLS
5 Achievement	. Desired levels of results out-puts and re-source inputs were reached.	. Good work! You have demonstrated your effectiveness. Your goal is to increase or maintain this effectiveness while decreasing the resources required to achieve these outcomes.
4 Transfer	. Recipients transferred content to performance of their task. . Goals were not achieved.	. You were able to impact recipient task performance. However, you may need to improve your skills in the following areas: - Identifying Key Result Areas - Setting Goal Levels - Identifying Contextual Tasks
3 Application	. Recipients applied their skills in a simulation. . Recipients failed to transfer.	. At the completion of training, your recipients reached skill mastery but failed to transfer the skills to the context. You may need to improve your skills in the following areas: - Identifying Contextual Tasks - Analyzing Contextual Barriers - Establishing Training Objectives - Developing Training Activities (In particular, the development of application exercises) You may also want to review additional skill areas listed above in Level 4.

Continued . . .

Table 14 (Continued)

UNDERSTANDING ASSESSMENT DATA: SETTING PERSONAL SKILL GOALS

ASSESSMENT LEVEL ACHIEVED	IMPLICATIONS	POTENTIAL DEFICITS IN INSTRUCTIONAL INTERVENTION SKILLS
2 Acquisition	. Recipients acquired the content. . Recipients were unable to apply the content.	Your recipients performed the skills but were unable to apply them to the dimensions of the training objective. You may need to improve your skills in the following areas: - Identifying Skills, Steps, and Supportive Knowledge - Developing Training Activities (In particular, the development of application exercises) You may also want to review additional skill areas listed previously in Level 3 and Level 4.
1 Process	. Recipients acted to process the training content. . Recipients failed to acquire the content.	Your recipients acted to process the training content but were unable to acquire it. You most likely need to improve your skills in the following areas: - Planning the Training Delivery (Developing training activities and selecting media) - Identifying Skills, Steps, and Supportive Knowledge You may also want to review additional skill areas listed previously in Levels 2, 3, and 4.

Continued . . .

Table 14 (Continued)

UNDERSTANDING ASSESSMENT DATA: SETTING PERSONAL SKILL GOALS

ASSESSMENT LEVEL ACHIEVED	IMPLICATIONS	POTENTIAL DEFICITS IN INSTRUCTIONAL INTERVENTION SKILLS
No Achievement	. Recipients failed to act to process the training content.	You most likely need to improve your skills in the following areas: **DESIGN:** - Planning the Training Delivery (In particular, building in opportunities for trainee processing within the plan) **DELIVERY:** - Content Processing Skills - Interpersonal Processing Skills You may also want to review all other skills previously mentioned.

```
┌──────────────────────────────────────────────────┐
│                                                  │
│  EXPLORING ──────▶ UNDERSTANDING ──────▶ ACTING  │
│      ▲                                     │     │
│      └─────────────────────────────────────┘     │
│                                                  │
└──────────────────────────────────────────────────┘
```

What Is Acting?

The final processing step is to act to achieve the goals resulting from our exploration of the assessment data. We now know: "Where We Are" and "Where We Want Or Need To Be." Next, we must determine: **"How To Get There."** Acting involves developing and implementing a plan for achieving our goals.

How Are Plans Developed?

We should already know how to develop an action plan. Developing an action plan is similar to developing skill steps. We simply identify and order the steps for achieving our goals. The key principle of acting is that our actions are more likely to be productive when they are systematic. The more systematic we are in our own learning programs, the more systematic our training recipients will be.

```
┌──────────────────────────────────────────────────┐
│                                                  │
│   REMEMBER . . .                                 │
│                                                  │
│   INSTRUCTIONAL TECHNOLOGISTS MUST BE            │
│   PRODUCTIVE, LIFE-LONG LEARNERS.  IF WE         │
│   STOP LEARNING, OUR TRAINEES WILL STOP          │
│   LEARNING.                                      │
│                                                  │
└──────────────────────────────────────────────────┘
```

What Happens After Acting?

Notice that the $E \longrightarrow U \longrightarrow A$ process begins over again after we have acted. When we act to achieve our goals, new assessment data are automatically generated. We then explore, understand, and act on these new data.

APPENDIX
FAVORABILITY SCALING

What Is Favorability Scaling?

Favorability scaling is a process which enables us to objectify or quantify subjective concepts or experiences.

Why Is Favorability Scaling Important?

Favorability scaling allows us to define subjective concepts or experiences in terms that are:

OBSERVABLE • MEASURABLE • VERIFIABLE

This conversion process, therefore, enables us to use observable, measurable, and verifiable data to assess achievement of subjective goals or performance standards.

How Is Favorability Scaling Done?

Favorability scaling involves three major steps. These steps are as follows:

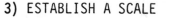

FAVORABILITY SCALING

3) ESTABLISH A SCALE

2) DEFINE THE CONCEPT/ EXPERIENCE

1) LABEL THE SUBJECTIVE CONCEPT/EXPERIENCE

This section describes each of these three steps, gives an example of using these three steps in an instructional evaluation context, and provides the reader with an opportunity to practice the steps with his or her own subjective concepts or experiences.

Step 1:
  Labeling

The first step in objectifying a subjective concept or experience is to clearly label the concept or experience.

The main consideration in completing the first step is that the label should be meaningful from the frame of reference of the person or group whose subjective concept or experience we are training to objectify.

Example:
  Labeling

The designer of a supervisory training course was concerned with the satisfaction of the manager whose supervisors were to take the course. The designer worked with the manager to find out what training outcomes would make the manager feel satisfied with the course.

The following interaction took place between the manager and instructional designer:

> **MANAGER:** "Training has to be useful."
>
> **DESIGNER:** "Useful for what?"
>
> **MANAGER:** "Useful on the job, useful in their actual day-to-day work."

At the end of their discussion, the manager and the designer agreed to label the manager's concept of training outcome as "on-the-job usefulness."

Step 2:
  Defining

The second step in objectifying a subjective concept or experience is to define the concept or experience in terms of one dimension or symbolic indicator of that concept or experience.

Again, the dimension or indicator must be one that is meaningful from the frame of reference of the person or group whose subjective concept or experience we are trying to objectify.

Continued . . .

Step 2:
  Defining
  (Continued)

In addition to being based on the "subject's" frame of reference, the dimension or indicator selected must be:

CRITERION	EXPLANATION
Observable	An observable indicator can be seen or sensed by a human being or a device created by a human being.
Measurable	A measurable indicator has differing levels to which labels or numbers can be assigned.
Verifiable	A verifiable indicator can be observed and measured by more than one human being.

Can Multiple
Indicators
Be Defined?

If several dimensions or indicators are found to be equally meaningful, then each one should form the basis of a separate favorability scale. In these cases, multiple favorability scales would be developed.

Example:
  Defining

The designer of the supervisory training course worked with the manager to define "on-the-job usefulness" in the form of an indicator that would:

- Be meaningful to the manager
          - AND -
- Be observable, measurable, and verifiable.

The following interaction took place between the manager and instructional designer:

DESIGNER: "What behavior of your supervisors will make you feel that the training is proving to be useful in your supervisors' day-to-day work?"

MANAGER: "If they start using the skills from the course in their regular work activities."

Continued . . .

Example:
   Defining
   (Continued)

Since the course dealt with specific supervisory interpersonal skills of attending, responding, personalizing, and initiating with employees, the manager and the designer agreed to operationally define "on-the-job usefulness" of the course as:

> The degree to which the trained supervisors use their new interpersonal skills with their employees in the normal work setting.

Step 3:
   Scaling

The third step in objectifying a subjective concept or experience is to establish a scale of levels for the dimension or indicator in terms of time or amount.

Again, as throughout this process, an important consideration is the frame of reference of the person or group whose subjective concept or experience we are trying to objectify. Two different individuals or groups might develop vastly different scales in terms of quantities that were meaningful to them.

This third step involves following four substeps:

Substep 3.1: Establish the **Most Favorable** level of the dimension or indicator.

Substep 3.2: Establish the **Least Favorable** level of the dimension or indicator.

Substep 3.3: Establish the **Minimally Acceptable** or middle level of the dimension or indicator.

Substep 3.4: Establish **Remaining Levels** of the dimension or indicator.

Substep 3.1:
 Establishing
 Most Favorable
 Level

To set the most favorable level of the scale, the individual or group whose concept or experience we are trying to objectify must answer the question:

Question: What is the **Ideal** level (in terms of time or amount) of this dimension or indicator?

Other ways of asking this question are:

**Alternate
Question:** What is the best that you could hope for on this dimension?

- OR -

**Alternate
Question:** What would be a double plus (++) on this indicator?

Example:
 Establishing
 Most Favorable
 Level

The designer of the supervisory training course worked with the manager to set an **Ideal** or **Most Favorable** level of the agreed-upon indicator of "on-the-job usefulness" of the course.

The following interaction took place between the manager and the instructional designer:

DESIGNER: "What would be the ideal or double plus (++) level of your supervisors using their new interpersonal skills with their employees in their work settings?"

MANAGER: "I would like them to use the skills in every interaction with an employee, but that may be a little unrealistic."

DESIGNER: "That's OK, the most favorable level of the scale should be the very best you could hope for or the most desirable level of the indicator. Let's tentatively set the top level of your favorability scale as:

> **++**
> Using interpersonal skills in every interaction with an employee in the work setting.

Substep 3.2: Establishing Least Favorable Level	To set the least favorable level of the scale, the individual or group whose concept or experience we are trying to objectify must answer the question:

<u>Question:</u>   What is the **Worst** level or least desirable level (in terms of time or amount) of this dimension or indicator?

Other ways of asking this question are:

<u>Alternate</u>   What is a totally unacceptable level of this
<u>Question:</u>   dimension?

- OR -

<u>Alternate</u>   What would be a double minus (--) on this
<u>Question:</u>   indicator?

<u>Example:</u> Establishing Least Favorable Level	The designer of the supervisory training course worked with the manager to establish the lowest or **Least Favorable** level of the agreed-upon indicator of "on-the-job usefulness" of the course.

The following interaction took place between the manager and the instructional designer.

DESIGNER: "What would be the least desirable or double minus (--) level of supervisor use of interpersonal skills?"

MANAGER: "If they don't use what they learned at all."

DESIGNER: "Let's tentatively set the lowest level of your favorability scale as:

> Not using interpersonal skills at all in interaction with employees in the work setting.

Substep 3.3:
    Establishing
    Minimally
    Acceptable
    Level

To set the minimally acceptable level of the scale, the individual or group whose concept or experience we are trying to objectify must answer the question:

Question: What is the barely satisfactory or **Minimally OK** level (in terms of time or amount) of this dimension or indicator?

Other ways of asking this question are:

Alternate   What is the neutral (0) level of this dimen-
Question: sion?
                              - OR -
Alternate   What is the level of this indicator that is
Question: neither positive nor negative (+/-)?

___

Example:
    Establishing
    Minimally
    Acceptable
    Level

The designer of the supervisory training course worked with the manager to set a minimally acceptable level of the agreed-upon indicator of "on-the-job usefulness" of the course.

The following interaction took place between the manager and the instructional designer.

DESIGNER: "What would be the minimally satisfactory level of supervisor use of interpersonal skills on the job?"

MANAGER: "After this training, I would be dissatisfied if the supervisors did not use their new interpersonal skills at least once a day in interactions with their employees."

DESIGNER: "So the middle or neutral level of your favorability scale could be:

+---+
| **+/-** |
| Using interpersonal skills at least once |
| per day in interactions with employees |
| in the work setting. |
+---+

___

Substep 3.4:
Establishing
Remaining
Levels
(Optional)

Completing Substeps 3.1, 3.2, and 3.3 will provide you with a three-point scale of an observable, measurable, and verifiable indicator of a subjective concept or experience.

Often, it will be desirable to establish additional points on the scale which indicate varying degrees of favorability. To develop a five-point or five-level scale, we simply specify levels in between the three anchor levels described in Substeps 3.1, 3.2, and 3.3.

To fill in these additional levels, the individual or group whose subjective concept or experience we are trying to objectify must answer the following questions:

Question: What level of the dimension or indicator is halfway between **Ideal** and **Minimally Acceptable**? (+)

- AND -

Question: What level of the dimension or indicator is halfway between **Minimally Acceptable** and **Least Favorable**? (-)

Example:
Establishing
Remaining
Levels

The designer of the supervisory course worked with the manager to set additional levels of the agreed-upon indicator of "on-the-job usefulness" of the course.

The following interaction took place between the manager and instructional designer:

DESIGNER: "What level of interpersonal skill use would be better than minimally acceptable but less than ideal?"

MANAGER: "Several times a day would be good."

DESIGNER: "And what level would be less than satisfactory but better than the least desirable level?"

MANAGER: "Oh, using the skills a little bit. Less than once a day would be better than not at all."

DESIGNER: "OK, then, let's take a look at your entire favorability scale:

Continued . . .

Example:	LEVELS		
Establishing Remaining Levels (Continued)	5	+ +	Using interpersonal skills in every inter-action with an employee in the work setting.
	4	+	Using interpersonal skills several times a day in interactions with employees in the work setting.
	3	+/-	Using interpersonal skills at least once per day in interactions with employees in the work setting.
	2	-	Using interpersonal skills less than once per day in interactions with employees in the work setting.
	1	- -	Not using interpersonal skills at all in interactions with employees in the work setting."

DESIGNER: "The question is this: Does this scale adequately measure your personal concept of this on-the-job usefulness of the supervisory training course?"

MANAGER: "If we collect data and apply this scale to those data, I will be comfortable that we are measuring my concept of the on-the-job usefulness of this course. Also, if the average score of the supervisory group is at Level 3 or above after training, I will be satisfied with the overall impact of the course."

Introduction   You may want to practice developing a favorability scale. To do so, try to develop a scale for a personal experience within a living (home), learning (training), or working context. For example, you may want to develop a scale for objectifying a subjective experience such as job contentment. Remember to complete the following steps:

STEP	
1	**LABEL** your subjective experience
2	**DEFINE** your experience in observable, measurable, and verifiable terms.
3	**SCALE** your experience by . . .
	. First, establishing the most favorable level (++).
	. Second, establishing the least favorable level (--).
	. Third, establishing the minimally acceptable or middle level (+/-).
	. Fourth, establishing the remaining two levels (+)(-). (This substep is optional.)

The following pages present a job aid that can be used when developing your favorability scale. You may also want to use this job aid when developing your assessment scales.

DEVELOPING A FAVORABILITY SCALE

STEP 1:
    LABEL

The name or label for the subjective concept/experience to be objectified is:

- -

✓ CHECK STEP: ☐   The concept/experience is stated in the subject's own terms.

STEP 2:
    DEFINE

One key dimension or indicator of this concept/experience is:

- -

✓ CHECK STEPS: The indicator is:

    ☐ OBSERVABLE   ☐ MEASURABLE   ☐ VERIFIABLE

    ☐   Again, the indicator is the one that the subject feels is important.

Continued . . .

DEVELOPING A FAVORABILITY SCALE

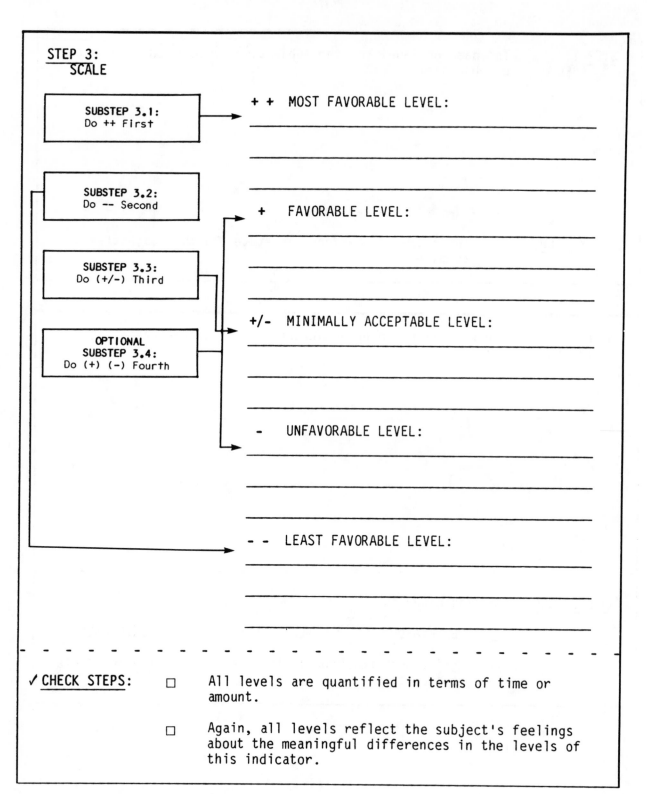

STEP 3:
SCALE

SUBSTEP 3.1:
Do ++ First

++ MOST FAVORABLE LEVEL:
_____
_____
_____

SUBSTEP 3.2:
Do -- Second

+ FAVORABLE LEVEL:
_____
_____
_____

SUBSTEP 3.3:
Do (+/-) Third

+/- MINIMALLY ACCEPTABLE LEVEL:
_____
_____
_____

OPTIONAL
SUBSTEP 3.4:
Do (+) (-) Fourth

- UNFAVORABLE LEVEL:
_____
_____
_____

-- LEAST FAVORABLE LEVEL:
_____
_____
_____

✓ CHECK STEPS: ☐ All levels are quantified in terms of time or amount.

☐ Again, all levels reflect the subject's feelings about the meaningful differences in the levels of this indicator.

**Can More Than
One Scale Be
Used?**

Frequently, it will be useful to develop several different scales to measure different dimensions or indicators of a subjective concept or experience.

Each scale is developed according to the steps outlined in the previous section.

**What If All
Scales Are
Not Equally
Important?**

Often, different dimensions or indicators of a concept or experience will <u>not</u> be of equal importance to the individual or group whose concept or experience we are trying to objectify.

If multiple scales are needed <u>and</u> the dimensions or indicators are of unequal importance, <u>then</u> a subjective weighting procedure can be used to capture the "subject's" frame of reference on the varying importance of the different scales. This procedure is referred to as differential weighting of multiple scales.

**How Are
Weighted Scales
Developed
And Used?**

Assigning differential weights to multiple scales must be done in interaction with the individual or group whose concepts or experiences we are trying to objectify. Weights from 10 (**Very** important) to 1 (**Not Very** important) can be assigned to each scaled dimension or indicator. Then scores on each scale can be multiplied by the appropriate weight to give a <u>weighted score</u>. The weighted score reflects the <u>relative</u> importance of the score in relation to scores on other scales.

**Example:
 Using
 Differential
 Weighted
 Scales**

The designer of the supervisory training course worked with the manager (see steps in previous section) to develop three favorability scales for three different indicators of "on-the-job usefulness" of the course.

Table 15 presents the three scales that were developed based on the manager's personal concept of on-the-job usefulness.

During the process of developing these scales, the manager indicated that the first scale was most important.

The designer asked the manager to assign a weight from 10 (very important) to 1 (not very important) to each of the three scales.

Continued . . .

Table 15.

ON-THE-JOB USEFULNESS OF TRAINING:
FAVORABILITY SCALES OF MANAGER A

LEVELS	SCALE 1 (Actual Use of Skills)	SCALE 2 (Reported Utility)	SCALE 3 (Employee Reports)
5 + +	Using interpersonal skills in every interaction	Supervisor reports that skills are useful on the job all of the time	75% or more of the supervisor's employees report improved relations with the supervisor
4 +	Using interpersonal skills several times a day	Supervisor reports that skills are useful on the job most of the time	60%-74% of the supervisor's employees report improved relations with the supervisor
3 +/-	Using interpersonal skills at least once per day	Supervisor reports that skills are useful on the job some of the time	50%-59% of the supervisor's employees report improved relations with the supervisor
2 -	Using interpersonal skills less than once per day	Supervisor reports that skills are not very useful on the job	25%-49% of the supervisor's employees report improved relations with the supervisor
1 - -	Not using interpersonal skills at all	Supervisor reports that skills are not at all useful on the job	Less than 25% of the supervisor's employees report improved relations with the supervisor

Example:
  Using
  Differential
  Weighted Scales
  (Continued)

The manager selected the following weights:

SCALE	WEIGHT
1	10
2	5
3	7

After the training and the post-training data collection activities, the supervisors' scores on the three scales were tabulated.

Table 16 shows how the weightings were used to give the manager a single composite "on-the-job usefulness" score for each supervisor. The composite score reflected both the manager's subjective frame of reference in developing the scales and her subjective frame of reference regarding the relative importance of the three indicators.

Table 16.

ON-THE-JOB USEFULNESS OF TRAINING:
SUPERVISORS' POST-TRAINING SCORES

SUPERVISOR	SCALE 1			SCALE 2			SCALE 3			COMPOSITE SCORE
	SCORE	WEIGHT	WGHTD. SCORE	SCORE	WEIGHT	WGHTD. SCORE	SCORE	WEIGHT	WGHTD. SCORE	
A	3	10	30	4	5	20	4	7	28	78
B	3	10	30	4	5	20	4	7	28	78
C	4	10	40	5	5	25	5	7	35	100
D	2	10	20	2	5	10	1	7	7	37
E	3	10	30	3	5	15	5	7	35	80
F	4	10	40	2	5	10	5	7	35	85
G	4	10	40	3	5	15	5	7	35	90
H	2	10	20	4	5	20	3	7	21	61
I	2	10	20	3	5	15	2	7	14	49

Average Composite Score: 73.11
Total Possible Composite Score: 110
Minimally Acceptable Composite Score: 66

**What Are
Developmental
Scales?**

As used in this series, developmental scales are a variation of favorability scaling.

A developmental scale has three primary characteristics:

- **BUILDING BLOCKS:** The scale reflects the sequential building blocks or <u>developmental</u> steps of the concept being scaled.

- **CUMULATIVE:** Each level of the scale incorporates the levels below.

- **BEHAVIORAL INDICES:** Behavioral indices are defined for each level of the scale.

**How Are
Developmental
Scales
Established?**

Developmental scales are established by completing the following three steps:

<u>STEP</u>	
1	**LABEL** your desired outcome.
2	**IDENTIFY** and **ORDER** the building blocks that lead up to the outcome. These become the levels within the scale.
3	**DEFINE** behavioral indices for each building block or level.

**Example:
Developmental
Scale**

Table 17 presents an example of a developmental scale used in this volume. Remember that any given level of the scale incorporates all the levels below that given level. For example, a level 3 rating indicates that levels 1, 2, and 3 have been achieved.

Table 17.

EXAMPLE DEVELOPMENTAL SCALE

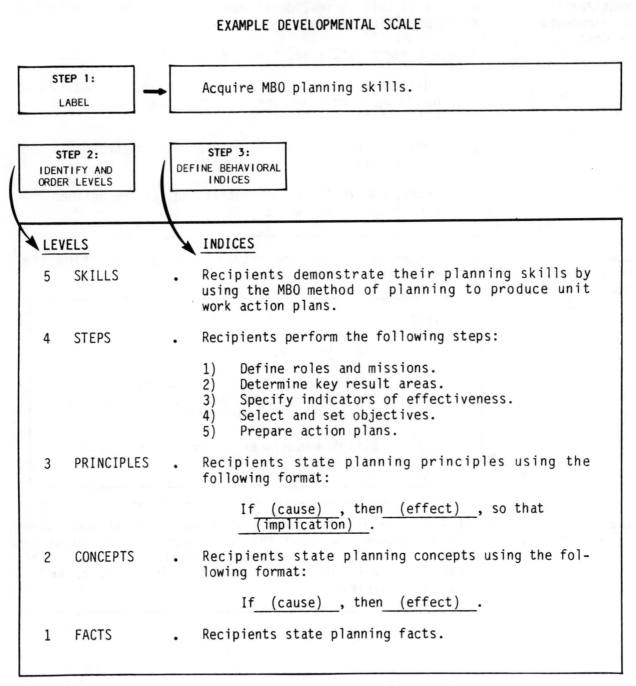

| STEP 1: LABEL | → | Acquire MBO planning skills. |

| STEP 2: IDENTIFY AND ORDER LEVELS | STEP 3: DEFINE BEHAVIORAL INDICES |

LEVELS **INDICES**

5 SKILLS . Recipients demonstrate their planning skills by using the MBO method of planning to produce unit work action plans.

4 STEPS . Recipients perform the following steps:

    1) Define roles and missions.
    2) Determine key result areas.
    3) Specify indicators of effectiveness.
    4) Select and set objectives.
    5) Prepare action plans.

3 PRINCIPLES . Recipients state planning principles using the following format:

    If (cause) , then (effect) , so that (implication) .

2 CONCEPTS . Recipients state planning concepts using the following format:

    If (cause) , then (effect) .

1 FACTS . Recipients state planning facts.

142

Key Principle

The key principle in favorability scaling is that everything depends on accurately representing the subject's frame of reference in terms that are:

> OBSERVABLE • MEASURABLE • VERIFIABLE

If this principle is adhered to, the designer/evaluator will succeed in the delicate process of objectifying or quantifying subjective concepts or experiences.

Interpersonal Skills

Basic interpersonal skills are the underlying skills needed by anyone who is working with an individual or group to objectify their subjective concepts or experiences. It is the effective use of interpersonal skills that enables us to fully enter and understand the frame of reference of another person or group.

It is this depth of understanding which then enables us to work with others to objectify or quantify their unique concepts or experiences of the world.

Steps In Scaling

Following are the major steps in favorability scaling and developmental scaling:

FAVORABILITY SCALING:

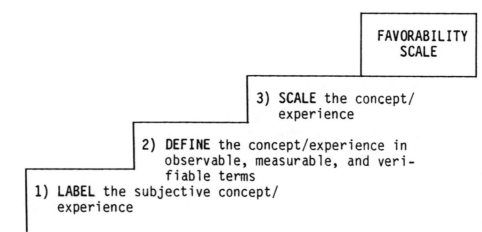

FAVORABILITY SCALE

3) SCALE the concept/ experience

2) DEFINE the concept/experience in observable, measurable, and verifiable terms

1) LABEL the subjective concept/ experience

Continued . . .

Steps In
Scaling
(Continued)

DEVELOPMENTAL SCALING:

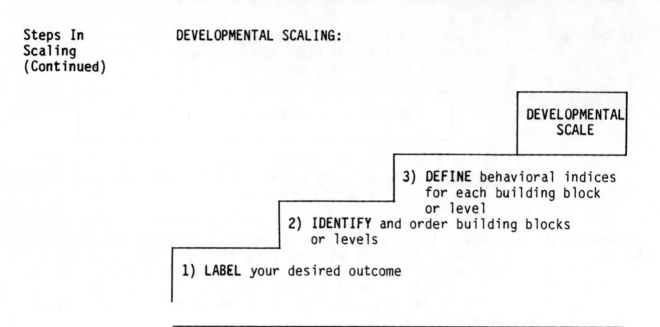

DEVELOPMENTAL
SCALE

3) **DEFINE** behavioral indices
for each building block
or level

2) **IDENTIFY** and order building blocks
or levels

1) **LABEL** your desired outcome

GLOSSARY

Application Evaluation: An assessment that measures whether or not training recipients can use the training content in work simulations.

Achievement Evaluation: An assessment that measures whether or not training recipients have achieved the productivity goals of their work units.

Acquisition Evaluation: An assessment that measures whether or not training recipients have acquired the training content.

Acting: The process used by training recipients to achieve their personal learning goals.

Components: Nouns in a training objective which describe persons, data, or things involved in performing the task/skill behavior ("who").

Concepts: Descriptions of how the various facts affect one another, often expressed in cause-and-effect relationships ("If. . ., then. . .").

Conditions: Adverbial phrases in a training objective describing the context in which the behavior takes place ("where"), the timeline for performing the behavior ("when"), and the purposes to be achieved by performing the behavior ("why").

Consulting Intervention: An intervention with the purpose of refining the productivity mission so that strategic plans can be developed.

Content: The steps, substeps, and supportive knowledge to be delivered to training recipients.

Content Development: Identification of the steps and knowledge required to achieve the training objectives.

Context: The work environment in which the recipients will be expected to perform task or skill behaviors.

Contextual Barriers: Any source which prevents the performance of the process tasks.

Contextual Tasks: The groups of work activities that must be performed to achieve the productivity goals.

Delivery Plan: The training activities, methods, and media to be used for ensuring the effective delivery of the training content.

Developmental Scale: A cumulative scale is a variation of favorability scaling that reflects the sequential building blocks or developmental steps of concepts being scaled (see favorability scaling).

Do: Training method that provides recipients with the opportunity to actually do the task/skill behavior.

DO Steps: The major steps the trainees will need to do to perform the task or skill.

DO Substeps: Sub-behaviors which, when added together, will lead to the performance of a DO step.

Enabling Task: A task necessary to support a process task.

Exercise: Element of content organization in which the training recipients practice the tasks or skills.

Exploring: The process used by training recipients to diagnose themselves in relation to the training content.

Facts: The components, functions, and processes of the training objective or step.

Favorability Scaling: A process which enables designers/evaluators to objectify or quantify subjective concepts or experiences.

Functions: Verbs in a training objective which describe the desired behavioral outcomes of the instructional intervention ("what").

Goal Level: Determination of the amount of change desired to occur in a key result area as a result of the training intervention.

Inputs: People, information, and/or capital resources which are used to accomplish the productivity mission.

Intervention: The process of initiating change.

Involving: The training recipients' physical behaviors of attending, observing, and listening.

Key Result Areas: The few organizational outputs that are critical to the achievement of the productivity mission.

Media: Vehicles or methods trainers use to deliver training content.

Organizational Components: The resource, production, marketing, and distribution segments of the organization.

Outputs: The finished products, services, and/or benefits resulting from the achievement of a goal.

Overview: Element of content organization in which images are shared with the training recipients on the content and its importance.

Preferred Courses of Action: The courses of action which maximize the probability of achieving strategic goals while minimizing the costs.

Presentation: Element of content organization in which content is presented so that recipients can learn the tasks or skills and accomplish the training objectives.

Principles: Descriptions of how and why something works, usually dealing with the implications of the cause-and-effect relationships of the concepts ("If. . ., then. . ., so that. . .").

Processes: Adverbial phrases that modify the functions of a training objective to describe the means by which the task/skill behavior is performed to reach the desired outcome ("how").

Process Tasks: The groups of work activities that must be performed by delivery, supervisory, and management personnel to achieve the productivity goals.

Productivity Achievement: The training recipients' achievement of productivity goals (i.e., the comparison of results outputs and resource inputs).

Productivity Goal: The desired outputs and anticipated levels of resource inputs.

Productivity Mission: A statement of goals for a target population, emphasizing a comparison of results outputs with resource inputs.

Programmatic: Step-by-step procedures to achieve desired goals.

Qualitative Goals: Desired outputs stated in terms of accuracy, functionality, or initiative.

Quantitative Goals: Desired outputs stated in terms of volume, rate, or timeliness.

Recipient: The individual who is to receive the training intervention.

Return-on-Investment (ROI): Ratio of the increments in results brought about by the added resource investments.

Review: Element of content organization in which content is reviewed in order to get an index of what the recipients do and do not know about the content to be addressed.

ROPES: Acronym for the content organization elements of Review, Overview, Presentation, Exercise, and Summary.

Show: Training method that demonstrates to the recipients how to do the task/skill behavior.

Skill Objectives: Those objectives that focus on the skills or behavioral objectives underlying the performance of contextual tasks.

Skills: Observable and repeatable behavior.

Standards: Adverbial phrases in a training objective which describe, in absolute or relative terms, the desired level of excellence to be achieved in performing the task ("how well").

Steps: Those behaviors which, when added together, will lead to the accomplishment of the training objectives.

Strategic Components: The organizational units which share in the achievement of the mission.

Strategic Delivery: The presentation of the strategic plans to decision makers, during which the decision makers process and refine the plans.

Strategic Goals: Goals which support the achievement of a productivity mission.

Strategic Plans: Designs for implementing the preferred courses of action that enable the organization to achieve the strategic goals and the productivity mission.

Substeps: Those sub-behaviors which, when added together, will lead to the performance of a task/skill step.

Summary: Element of content organization in which content is summarized in order to get an index of what the recipients do and do not know about the tasks or skills following the training delivery.

Supportive Knowledge: Facts, concepts, and principles which are needed in order to perform a task or skill.

Task Objectives: Those objectives that focus primarily on the performance of specific contextual tasks.

Tell: Training method that informs the recipients about what task/skill behavior is to be done and how to do it.

THINK Steps: Questions for training recipients to answer before, during, and after completing a DO step or substep so they can monitor their own performance.

Training Delivery Plan: Vehicle used by the instructional technologist to provide training recipients with new tasks, skills, and knowledge. A training delivery plan organizes the content, establishes the training methods, and specifies the training media.

Training Methods: Didactic (tell), modeling (show), and exercise (do).

Transfer Evaluation: An assessment which measures whether or not training recipients use the training content (skills/knowledge) in the performance of their jobs.

Understanding: The process used by training recipients to establish their own personal learning goals.

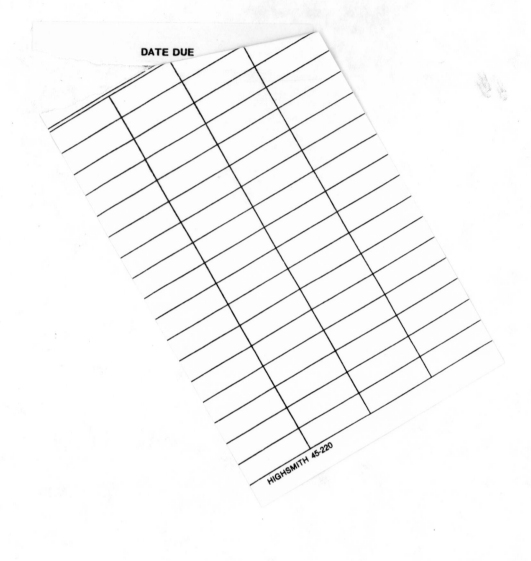

DATE DUE

HIGHSMITH 45-220